—Real Food —
Soups
and Smoothies
from your Blender

— Real Food —
Soups
and Smoothies
from your Blender

Sonia Allison

foulsham
LONDON • NEW YORK • TORONTO • SYDNEY

foulsham

The Publishing House, Bennetts Close, Cippenham,
Slough, Berkshire, SL1 5AP, England

ISBN 0-572-02498-3

Cover photograph by Peter Howard Smith

Printed in Great Britain by Mackays of Chatham plc, Chatham, Kent

Contents

Introduction

*V*ersatile, healthy, ideal for a quick snack or easy to serve with crusty bread for a main meal, the humble soup comes in so many guises – from a cooling summer-fruit refresher to a thick, spicy and warming winter dish. When I came to put together this new collection, I decided to give it an international flavour to make the most of all the delicious ways of serving soup around the world. Then, of course, I couldn't ignore the soup's cousin – the delicious smoothie. Nourishing, quick and tremendously tasty, they are just right for our hectic modern lifestyle.

Britain has more than her fair share of tomato, mushroom, chicken and oxtail soups and Scotch broth. But head to Holland in the winter and you'll be presented with more yellow pea soup – 'so thick your spoon will stand up in it' – than you'll know what to do with. Further north, in Denmark, Norway and Sweden, many other versions are on offer.

Finland has adopted from neighbouring Russia its bortsch or beetroot (red beet) soup, along with its own array of soups using every imaginable fish from its unique network of some 60,000 local lakes and rivers. Russia's range of beetroot bortsches includes a glassy clear one in vivid dark red, sometimes served cold. Another group of Russian soups, called *shchi,* is based on leaves – perhaps cabbage, young nettles, sour-tasting sorrel, spinach or beetroot, or a mixture of greenery depending on the cook's mood. Nearby Poland also specialises in bortsch, which is frequently served with floats of *pierogi* (basically meat-filled ravioli) and traditional *chlodnik litewski* – white bortsch – which is a gem of a soup heavy with soured (dairy sour) cream, vegetables, cucumber, fresh chives and dill (dill weed), milk and hard-boiled (hard-cooked) eggs. The national summer favourite is sorrel soup, revered for its tangy taste and refreshing qualities. By contrast, in Central Europe, the Czech Republic has its own style of goulash soup (a hangover from the Austro-Hungarian Empire), a hefty onion soup containing dark rye bread, and a sustaining chicken soup with noodles.

Germany, predictably, goes in for beer soup, a winter breakfast soup with buttermilk, potato soup with or without paprika, and a rugged bean and vegetable soup native to Westphalia. For a touch more elegance, there are clear soups with tiny dumplings and a selection of cream soups. Over to Belgium, whose chervil soup and a soup with green eels bring tears of joy to any citizen's eye. For the rest of us, the country is renowned for its vegetable purée soups laden with butter and cream. France is closely associated with brown onion soup, vichyssoise and any number of fish soups, headed by Provençal bouillabaisse. Italy is renowned for its lively minestrone, fine consommés with ravioli or tiny pasta, the clear stracciatella (egg lace soup) with eggs and polenta, mussel soup and other fish soups jam-packed with a multitude of locally caught fish. Switzerland stays with comforting cheese soups combined with bread and wine – almost a fondue taste-alike – mixed vegetable soups with rice, and a green onion soup densely packed with snipped fresh chives to give it its emerald colour.

Austria loves dumplings – of whatever size and whether light or heavy – in clear soup and also goes in for stalwarts such as a combo of celeriac (celery root) and potato. There is also goulash soup full of meat or poultry and mild red paprika, bread soup and garlic soup amid a vast repertoire of other hot and cold specialities, with thoughtful seasoning and always tastefully presented. Hungary's great classic, apart from goulash soup, is *halaszle,* a soup packed with choice local fish such as carp, pike, perch and *kecsege* (a fish related to the sturgeon), and seasoned mightily with paprika and onion.

Bulgaria specialises in hot and cold yoghurt soups while Rumania has fanciful mixes of beef soup beaten with eggs, vegetable soups with ham and noodles, and a vast haricot (navy) bean soup – again called bortsch – with a cornucopia of vegetables including raw beetroot (red beet). Yugoslavia's most important soups are those based on fish, while Turkey has a rich and golden red lentil soup, another with tripe and something called wedding soup, a celebratory affair filled to the brim with meat, mixed vegetables, eggs and lemon. Greece is conservative where soup is concerned and her best known one is avogolemono, a lightish and mild chicken soup containing rice, eggs and lemon juice. But look hard and you'll probably be able to track down *kakavia,* which is similar to bouillabaisse, and other appetising soups based on chick peas (garbanzos), lentils and beans. Spain is renowned for chilled gazpachos, red ones with tomatoes and white ones with almonds and milk. Hot soups appear with fish and eggs. Portugal's national soup is *caldo verde,* or green cabbage, but she also has an engaging tomato soup and innumerable others using local meat, fish, seasonal vegetables, sausages, bacon, ham and spices such as cinnamon.

North Africa goes in for lentil soup, as does Turkey, along with throat-grabbing vegetable soups laced with spice and fire and dancing with chick peas and chillies. Examples are Algeria's *chorba hamra* and Morocco's *harira,* stuffed to the gunwales with fresh and dried vegetables, pasta and lamb and eaten to break the fast during the holy month of Ramadam. Even the rest of sun-baked Africa has a collection of soups that use local ingredients like okra (ladies' fingers), black-eyed beans and other dried pulses, squashes, yams, sweet potatoes, plantains, tomatoes, onions, garlic, seafood, peanuts, tapioca and sparing amounts of meat.

The Americas, Australia and New Zealand borrow much from Europe and the Far East and cleverly and convincingly adapt concepts and recipes to suit seasonal ingredients, climate and national tastes, producing a brilliant band of homespun classic soups or the now fashionable fusion, a combination of East and West.

Asia, from Thailand to China to Japan, has at least as many soups as everywhere else put together. India alone appears to be a non-soup-drinking nation unless you count dahl, a 'stew' of lentils and spices, usually eaten there as a meal with rice but thinned down to a liquid elsewhere and served as soup in Anglo-Indian restaurants. I doubt its authenticity.

This book offers more than a hundred innovative and easily made recipes, featuring both familiar tastes and foreign flavours. The rest of the world is never far away from our soup bowls.

Soups and Smoothies Storecupboard

*I*t is useful to carry a comprehensive range of ingredients at home in case you suddenly decide to make a soup or smoothie but have no time for shopping. Under each of the following headings you will find a list of useful items to keep on hand should the need arise. Apart from the usual storecupboard staples like flour and rice, salt and pepper, mustard and vinegars, there are many additions that take into account the recipes in this book.

Dry stores and packets

◇ Rice: fragrant Thai, brown or white basmati, brown rice flakes, imperial red
◇ Nuts: macadamia, almonds including flaked (slivered), pine nuts, pistachios, walnuts
◇ Pasta: rice noodles, quick-cook macaroni
◇ Grains and pulses: tapioca, barley, porridge oats, couscous, puy lentils, orange lentils, yellow split peas, butter (lima) beans
◇ Gelatine
◇ Stock (bouillon) powder or cubes: fish, chicken, beef, vegetable
◇ Sugar: white and brown
◇ Dried fruits: sultanas (golden raisins), raisins, apricots
◇ Flours: plain (all-purpose), potato flour (farina), cornflour (cornstarch)
◇ Seasonings: white and black pepper, salt

Canned and bottled foods

◇ Fish sauce
◇ Coconut milk
◇ Oils: olive, sunflower, sesame, groundnut (peanut)

◇ Alcohol: red, rosé and white wines, Campari, amaretto di saronno, apricot brandy, orange-flavoured liqueur, crème de cassis, crème de menthe, sparkling perry, sweet cider, medium sherry, Pernod or Ricard

◇ Fruit juices: passion, tropical, orange, apple, pineapple, peach, mango, custard apple, pink grapefruit, cranberry, sparkling red and white grape juice, tomato, carrot

◇ Cold drinks: lemonade, orangeade, dry ginger ale

◇ Crunchy peanut butter

◇ Beef consommé

◇ Pulses: red kidney beans, chick peas (garbanzos), mushy peas

◇ Preserves: orange marmalade, clear honey, set honey, caramel-flavoured syrup

◇ Vegetables: artichoke hearts, pimientos, tomatoes

◇ Tuna in brine

◇ Fruit: mandarin oranges, fruit cocktail, grapefruit segments, pears, assorted fruit fillings

◇ Pickled beetroot (red beet)

Herbs, flavourings and condiments

◇ Spices: mild curry powder, Madras curry powder, turmeric, saffron, tandoori spice mix, chilli powder, cinnamon, bay leaves, five-spice powder, garam masala, ground cumin, ground coriander (cilantro), ground cardamom, whole and ground allspice, mustard powder, nutmeg

◇ Cordials: ginger and lemon grass, elderflower, grenadine syrup

◇ Herbs: tarragon, thyme, sage, basil

◇ Flower waters: rose and orange

◇ Flavourings: anchovy essence (extract), mushroom ketchup (catsup), soy sauce, chilli sauce, Worcestershire sauce, Tabasco sauce (green and red), Angostura bitters, brown ketchup, creamed horseradish, English mustard, wholegrain mustard, Dijon mustard, juniper berries, pesto, mango chutney, redcurrant jelly (clear conserve), tahini, capers

◇ Vinegars: cider, sherry, malt, chilli, balsamic

◇ Dried vegetables: red chillies, sun-dried tomatoes, porcini mushrooms
◇ Purées (pastes): tomato, sun-dried tomato, chilli

Chilled foods

◇ Cheeses: Cheddar, Stilton, Parmesan, Mascarpone, Mozzarella, Feta
◇ Dairy: buttermilk, crème fraîche, soured (dairy sour) cream, full cream milk, skimmed milk, plain yoghurt, butter, custard sauce
◇ Herbs: red and green fresh chillies, fresh root ginger, garlic
◇ Juices: fresh lemon and lime
◇ Fruits: lemons, limes
◇ White bread

Frozen foods

◇ Prawns (shrimp)
◇ Lemon grass stalks
◇ Lime leaves
◇ Vanilla ice cream
◇ Sorbets
◇ Chestnuts
◇ Peas

Notes on the Recipes

◇ Do not mix metric, imperial and American measures. Follow one set only.

◇ All spoon measures are level unless otherwise stated: 1 tsp = 5 ml; 1 tbsp = 15 ml.

◇ Eggs are medium.

◇ Thoroughly wash all vegetables and fruit before use and, to remove pesticides from citrus fruit skins, scrub well with a brush under running water.

◇ Fish, poultry and meat should be rinsed before using in recipes and cooked and raw items must be kept well apart to prevent contamination and possible food poisoning.

◇ Fresh and frozen herbs have the most authentic flavours but, if unavailable, use half the quantity given of dried. There is no substitute for fresh parsley, coriander (cilantro) and dill (dill weed).

◇ Always use the oil specified in the recipe.

◇ Margarine may be substituted for butter, but check the packet to ensure it is suitable for the particular use.

◇ Preparation and cooking times are approximate.

◇ Use labour-saving kitchen appliances for speed such as a food processor for slicing, chopping and grinding. A mandolin also works well.

◇ When adding crème fraîche to soup, do not allow it to boil. The soup may be brought just up to boiling point, then quickly taken away from the heat.

◇ Saltiness can intensify after the soup has been made so adjust quantities to taste. You may find that chilled soups need more generous seasoning than hot soups. Add pepper to taste.

Chilled Savoury Soups

Savoury chilled soups, based mostly on vegetable combinations, are perfect for the summer months and make cooling and innovative meal starters for any occasion. The best-known favourites are gazpacho and vichyssoise, but just as refreshing are soups made from cucumber – fresh and sour – tomatoes, mushrooms, avocados, watercress, lettuce, fresh and canned or bottled (bell) peppers, spinach, beetroot (red beet) and peas.

Some of the soups in this section have foreign overtones but most use familiar and popular ingredients that are easily found in local food stores.

You may find that chilled soups need a little more seasoning than hot soups. Experiment until you get it right and use additional herbs if you prefer not to add too much salt.

Middle Eastern Tahini Soup with Chick Peas and Lemon

SERVES ABOUT 8

A gentle-tasting and cooling soup with a hint of spice that is great to serve before a barbecue or a weekend roast of lamb or chicken.

---

450 ml/¾ pt/2 cups tahini
600 ml/1 pt/2½ cups vegetable stock or water
Juice of 3 large lemons
2 garlic cloves, crushed
15 ml/1 tbsp finely chopped mint
Salt and freshly ground black pepper
Ice cubes
100 g/4 oz/⅔ cup canned chick peas (garbanzos)
A few sprigs of fresh parsley

---

① Blend together the tahini, stock or water, lemon juice and garlic.

② Stir in the mint and season to taste with salt and pepper.

③ Pour into bowls over ice cubes.

④ Divide the chick peas between the bowls, add a few parsley sprigs to each and serve.

PREPARATION TIME: 10 MINUTES

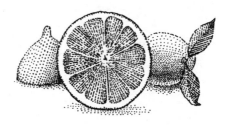

Sour Cucumber Soup
SERVES 4

A sharply sweet-sour soup to take the heat out of summer.

350 g/12 oz/5 cups pickled sweet-sour (dill) cucumbers,
   diced
225 g/8 oz unpeeled fresh cucumber
150 ml/¼ pt/⅔ cup sweet-sour cucumber water
300 ml/½ pt/1¼ cups cold water
45 ml/3 tbsp Pernod or Ricard
2 garlic cloves, crushed
Salt and freshly ground black pepper
90 ml/6 tbsp soured (dairy sour) cream or crème fraîche

① Blend the pickled and fresh cucumbers, cucumber water and cold water in two batches until very smooth. Pour into a bowl.

② Add the Pernod or Ricard and garlic and season to taste with salt and pepper.

③ Cover and chill thoroughly.

④ Before serving, stir the soup well, pour into bowls and top each one with a generous dollop of the soured cream or crème fraîche.

PREPARATION TIME: 15 MINUTES

Cucumber Soup with Garlic and Green Pepper Ribbons
SERVES 4

A fabulous-tasting soup in quiet and calming green.

1 medium cucumber, peeled and cubed
60 ml/4 tbsp chopped dill (dill weed)
2 garlic cloves, peeled
5 ml/1 tsp salt
450 ml/¾ pt/2 cups low-fat set yoghurt
1 small green (bell) pepper, seeded and cut into fine strips

① Place the cucumber, dill, garlic and salt in the blender and add half the yoghurt. Blend until smooth, then transfer to a bowl.

② Gently whisk in the remaining yoghurt.

③ Cover the bowl, then chill the soup thoroughly.

④ Before serving, stir the soup, pour into bowls and sprinkle each portion with the pepper strips.

PREPARATION TIME: 15 MINUTES

Bulgarian Yoghurt and Cucumber Soup with Walnuts
SERVES 4

Prepare as for Cucumber Soup with Garlic and Green Pepper Ribbons, but add 50 g/2 oz/½ cup of chopped walnuts with the dill (dill weed) and omit the pepper strips.

Chilled Carrot and Potato Soup with Orange Liqueur

SERVES 8

A delicate soup to enjoy on a hot summer's day.

---

700 g/1½ lb carrots, cut into large cubes
700 g/1½ lb potatoes, cut into large cubes
2 onions, sliced
1.5 litres/2½ pts/6 cups water
10 ml/2 tsp salt
60 ml/4 tbsp orange-flavoured liqueur
150 ml/¼ pt/⅔ cup crème fraîche
45 ml/3 tbsp chopped dill (dill weed)

---

① Place the carrots, potatoes and onions in a large saucepan with the water and salt. Bring to the boil.

② Lower the heat, cover and simmer for 30–40 minutes or until the vegetables are soft.

③ Remove from the heat and leave to cool.

④ When lukewarm, blend in two or three batches until smooth.

⑤ Transfer to a large bowl, cover and leave to cool completely, then chill for several hours.

⑥ Before serving, gently whisk in the liqueur and crème fraîche. Sprinkle each portion with the dill.

PREPARATION TIME: 30 MINUTES
COOKING TIME: 30–40 MINUTES

Guacamole Soup with Red Kidney Beans

SERVES 6

*A hot and spicy Mexican-style soup with a unique
and forceful flavour.*

---

400 g/14 oz/1 large can of red kidney beans
6 spring onions (scallions), sliced
2 ripe avocados, halved and stoned (pitted)
1 green chilli, halved and seeded
30 ml/2 tbsp tomato purée (paste)
Juice of 2 limes
5 ml/1 tsp salt
5 ml/1 tsp Tabasco sauce
600 ml/1 pt/2½ cups vegetable stock
30 ml/2 tbsp cider vinegar
To serve:
Tortilla chips

---

① Blend the contents of the can of kidney beans to a coarse purée.

② Add the remaining ingredients except half the stock and the vinegar and blend until semi-smooth.

③ Transfer to a large bowl and slowly whisk in the remaining stock.

④ Stir in the cider vinegar, then cover the bowl and chill for several hours until very cold.

⑤ Stir well before serving with tortilla chips.

PREPARATION TIME: 25 MINUTES

Watercress Soup with Onion and Celery
SERVES 4–6

A delightful pale green soup, its undercurrents of watercress and elderflower making a quiet and unusual statement. Definitely a cool customer!

150 g/5 oz watercress
2 onions, cut into chunks
3 celery sticks, thinly sliced
450 ml/¾ pt/2 cups full cream milk
450 ml/¾ pt/2 cups water
5 ml/1 tsp salt
30 ml/2 tbsp elderflower cordial

① Place all the ingredients except the elderflower cordial in a saucepan and bring to the boil, stirring.

② Lower the heat, cover and simmer for 30 minutes, stirring occasionally, until the vegetables are soft.

③ Remove from the heat and leave to cool.

④ When lukewarm, blend in two or three batches until smooth.

⑤ Transfer to a large bowl and stir in the elderflower cordial. Cover and chill.

⑥ Stir well before serving.

PREPARATION TIME: 15 MINUTES
COOKING TIME: 30 MINUTES

Watercress and Leek Cream Soup

SERVES 6–8

A light and refreshing soup with a creamy consistency.

---

1 large leek, halved lengthways and coarsely chopped
100 g/4 oz watercress
350 g/12 oz potatoes, peeled and diced
900 ml/1½ pts/3¾ cups water
150 ml/¼ pt/⅔ cup full cream milk
5–10 ml/1–2 tsp salt
150 ml/¼ pt/⅔ cup single (light) cream

---

① Place all the ingredients except the cream in a large saucepan and bring to the boil.

② Lower the heat, cover and simmer for 25–30 minutes or until the vegetables are very soft.

③ Remove from the heat and leave to cool completely.

④ Blend in two or three batches until smooth.

⑤ Transfer to a large bowl, cover and chill for several hours.

⑥ Stir in the cream before serving.

PREPARATION TIME: 15 MINUTES
COOKING TIME: 30 MINUTES

Pimiento Soup with Yoghurt, Mascarpone and Chilli

SERVES 6

A smart and characterful soup which is slightly sweet-sour and piquant. For maximum flavour, eat the soup within 24 hours of making it.

---

400 g/14 oz/1 large can of whole pimientos in water with added salt
125 g/4½ oz/generous ½ cup Mascarpone cheese
200 ml/7 fl oz/scant 1 cup plain yoghurt
350 ml/12 fl oz/1⅓ cups water
2.5–5 ml/½–1 tsp chilli powder
200 ml/7 fl oz/scant 1 cup tomato juice
30 ml/2 tbsp sherry vinegar
To serve:
Grated orange rind (optional)

---

① Tip the contents of the can of pimientos into the blender. Add the Mascarpone, yoghurt, water and chilli powder and blend until very smooth.

② Transfer to a bowl, add the tomato juice and vinegar and stir well. Cover and chill for several hours.

③ Stir well before serving sprinkled with a little grated orange rind, if liked.

PREPARATION TIME: 10 MINUTES

Spinach and Herbed Cheese Soup
SERVES 4–6

A smart affair, yet easy to make.

---

175 g/6 oz fresh baby leaf spinach
600 ml/1 pt/2½ cups vegetable stock
450 ml/¾ pt/2 cups skimmed milk
150 g/5 oz/⅔ cup full fat cream cheese with fines herbes
5–7.5 ml/1–1½ tsp salt

---

① Place the spinach, stock and milk in a large saucepan and bring to the boil.

② Lower the heat, cover and simmer for 10 minutes.

③ Remove from the heat and leave to cool completely.

④ Blend in two or three batches, adding the cheese, until smooth.

⑤ Pour into a large bowl and season to taste with the salt. Cover and chill for several hours.

⑥ Stir thoroughly before serving.

PREPARATION TIME: 10 MINUTES
COOKING TIME: 10 MINUTES

Oriental Mushroom and Rice Milk Soup

SERVES 6–8

A smoky-tasting soup, and very attractive with its colourful garnish.

---

500 g/18 oz mushrooms, broken into small pieces
30 ml/2 tbsp toasted sesame oil
900 ml/1½ pts/3¾ cups unflavoured rice milk
1 garlic clove, crushed
5–10 ml/1–2 tsp salt
15 ml/1 tbsp soy sauce
10 ml/2 tsp cornflour (cornstarch)
300 ml/½ pt/1¼ cups water
45 ml/3 tbsp snipped chives
15 ml/1 tbsp grated orange rind

---

① Fry (sauté) the mushrooms in the sesame oil in a large saucepan until tender.

② Mix in 600 ml/1 pt/2½ cups of the rice milk, the garlic, salt and soy sauce and bring to the boil, stirring.

③ Lower the heat, cover and simmer gently for 15 minutes.

④ Mix the cornflour to a smooth paste with a little of the remaining rice milk. Mix in the rest of the milk and the water, then pour into the saucepan.

⑤ Bring gently to the boil, stirring, then lower the heat and simmer for 2 minutes until thickened.

⑥ Remove from the heat and leave to cool completely.

⑦ Blend in two or three batches until smooth, then transfer to a large bowl. Cover and chill for several hours.

⑧ Stir before serving, sprinkling each portion with the chives and orange rind.

PREPARATION TIME: 15 MINUTES
COOKING TIME: 25 MINUTES

Chestnut Mushroom Soup with Garlic and Fried Walnuts

SERVES 4

An east-west combo with a diversity of flavours.

225 g/8 oz chestnut mushrooms, broken into pieces
4 garlic cloves, peeled and halved
300 ml/½ pt/1¼ cups milk
7.5 ml/1½ tsp salt
5 ml/1 tsp dried thyme
7.5 ml/1½ tsp ground cumin
300 ml/½ pt/1¼ cups water
15 g/½ oz/1 tbsp butter
5 ml/1 tsp olive oil
50 g/2 oz/½ cup shelled walnuts, broken into pieces

① Place the mushrooms and garlic in a pan with the milk, salt, thyme, cumin and water.

② Bring to the boil, then lower the heat, cover and simmer for 15 minutes.

③ Meanwhile, heat the butter gently in a separate pan with the oil until melted. Add the walnuts and fry (sauté) over a medium-low heat for 5 minutes.

④ Allow the soup to cool to lukewarm, then stir in the nuts.

⑤ Blend in two or three batches to a coarse purée. Transfer to a large bowl, cover and chill for several hours.

⑥ Stir well before serving.

PREPARATION TIME: 20 MINUTES
COOKING TIME: 20 MINUTES

Tomato and Carrot Soup with Basil and Mint

SERVES 4

An easy-to-make and almost instant soup with a stunning flavour and zippy tang.

---

400 g/14 oz/1 large can of tomatoes
400 g/14 oz/1 large can of sliced carrots in water
6 basil leaves
6 mint leaves
5 ml/1 tsp caster (superfine) sugar
5 ml/1 tsp salt
15 ml/1 tbsp brown sauce
300 ml/½ pt/1¼ cups chilled water

---

① Tip the contents of the cans of tomatoes and carrots into the blender.

② Add the remaining ingredients and blend until smooth.

③ Pour into a bowl, cover and chill thoroughly for several hours.

④ Stir before serving.

PREPARATION TIME: 10 MINUTES

Beetroot Soup with Tomatoes and Horseradish

SERVES 8

A cheerful soup with a striking personality.

---

450 g/1 lb ripe tomatoes, blanched, skinned and
  quartered
700 g/1½ lb cooked beetroot (red beet), peeled and cut
  into chunks
2 garlic cloves, peeled and halved
10 ml/2 tsp salt
30 ml/2 tbsp creamed horseradish
750 ml/1¼ pt/3 cups water
30 ml/2 tbsp cider vinegar
60 ml/4 tbsp crème fraîche

---

① Blend the tomatoes, beetroot and garlic in two batches until smooth.

② Transfer to a bowl and gently whisk in the salt, horseradish, water and vinegar.

③ Cover and chill for several hours until very cold.

④ Stir before serving, topping each portion with a swirl of the crème fraîche.

PREPARATION TIME: 20 MINUTES

Beetroot and Lemon Soup

SERVES 4–5

A refreshing slimline soup.

---

450 g/1 lb cooked beetroot (red beet), peeled and cubed
450 ml/¾ pt/2 cups water
Juice of 1 large lemon
1 garlic clove, sliced
5 ml/1 tsp salt
250 ml/8 fl oz/1 cup buttermilk

---

① Blend all the ingredients except the buttermilk until very smooth.

② Transfer to a bowl and gently whisk in the buttermilk. Cover and chill for several hours.

③ Stir before serving.

PREPARATION TIME: 10 MINUTES

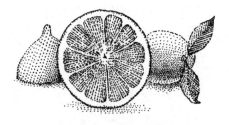

Gazpacho
SERVES 6

Spain's national soup is gloriously cooling in the heat. It can be eaten on its own or with a choice of any of the accompaniments I have listed.

---

450 g/1 lb ripe tomatoes, blanched, skinned and coarsely sliced
1–2 garlic cloves, peeled and each cut into 3
1 red (bell) pepper, halved, seeded and cut into strips
1 green pepper, halved, seeded and cut into strips
1 onion, chopped
½ unpeeled cucumber, diced
45 ml/3 tbsp tomato purée (paste)
10 ml/2 tsp caster (superfine) sugar
45 ml/3 tbsp olive oil
30 ml/2 tbsp sherry vinegar
2 large slices of white bread, crumbed
300 ml/½ pt/1¼ cups water
Optional accompaniments:
Coarsely chopped cucumber, diced red and green peppers, chopped hard-boiled (hard-cooked) egg, coarsely chopped red onion, croûtons

---

① Place the tomatoes, garlic, pepper strips, onion, cucumber, tomato purée and sugar in a large bowl and mix together.

② Blend in two batches until smooth, then return to the bowl.

③ Whisk in the olive oil and vinegar, then gently mix in the breadcrumbs and water.

④ Cover and chill for several hours until very cold.

⑤ Stir before serving with dishes of your chosen additions handed separately.

PREPARATION TIME: 20–25 MINUTES
(LONGER IF ADDITIONS ARE INCLUDED)

Tomato Consommé with Sherry
SERVES 6

A lovely summer soup and great for entertaining as it can be made well ahead and chilled until needed.

20 ml/4 tsp powdered gelatine
30 ml/2 tbsp cold water
30 ml/2 tbsp hot water
700 g/1½ lb tomatoes, skinned and quartered
5 ml/1 tsp green Tabasco sauce
10 ml/2 tsp Worcestershire sauce
5 ml/1 tsp salt
30 ml/2 tbsp medium-dry sherry
20 ml/4 tsp snipped fresh chives

① Place the gelatine in a saucepan. Add the cold water and leave to soften for 5 minutes. Stir in the hot water, then melt over the lowest possible heat until clear.

② Place the tomatoes, Tabasco and Worcestershire sauces, salt and sherry in the blender and blend until smooth.

③ Transfer to a bowl and stir in the warm melted gelatine. Cover and chill until softly set and really cold.

④ Break up with a spoon and serve with a sprinkling of the chives on each portion.

PREPARATION TIME: 20 MINUTES

Vichyssoise
SERVES 6–8

This lovely soup is not seen about as much as it used to be but is far too good to be shelved in the name of progress! An American invention – despite its French name – this golden oldie is a smooth, unashamedly rich and irresistible 1920s classic.

4 young leeks
1 onion, peeled and sliced
450 g/1 lb potatoes, peeled and cubed
1 litre/1¾ pts/4¼ cups water
10–15 ml/2–3 tsp salt
300 ml/½ pt/1¼ cups whipping cream
60 ml/4 tbsp snipped fresh chives

① Discard most of the green part from the leeks. Slit the remaining white parts lengthways and wash thoroughly between the leaves. Slice.

② Place in a large saucepan with the onion, potatoes, water and salt and bring gently to the boil.

③ Lower the heat, cover and simmer gently for 50–60 minutes or until the vegetables are very soft.

④ Leave to cool to lukewarm, then blend in two or three batches until very smooth.

⑤ Transfer to a large bowl and gently whisk in the cream. Cover and chill for several hours.

⑥ Stir before serving sprinkled with the chives.

PREPARATION TIME: 20 MINUTES
COOKING TIME: 1¼ HOURS

Pea and Mint Soup
SERVES 4

*An elegant soup, although it has only four ingredients.
You can substitute marrowfat peas for the mushy peas if
you prefer.*

400 g/14 oz/1 large can of mushy peas
5 ml/1 tsp chopped fresh mint
600 ml/1 pt/2½ cups vegetable stock
60 ml/4 tbsp whipping cream
Thinly sliced mint leaves, to garnish

① Blend the peas, chopped mint and stock until smooth.

② Transfer to a saucepan, stir in the cream and heat gently without boiling.

③ Leave to cool to lukewarm, then cover and chill.

④ Stir before serving, sprinkled with the sliced mint.

PREPARATION TIME: 5 MINUTES
COOKING TIME: 5 MINUTES

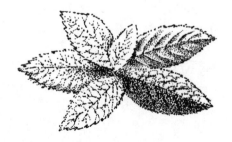

Lettuce, Garlic and Feta Soup
SERVES 6

Make this soup with fully grown summer lettuces for the best results and indulge in an off-beat, chilled soup with a creamy texture and fine flavour.

---

3 round lettuces, finely shredded
3 garlic cloves, halved
1 litre/1¾ pts/4¼ cups water
10 ml/2 tsp caster (superfine) sugar
7.5 ml/1½ tsp salt
30 ml/2 tbsp potato flour (farina)
150 ml/¼ pt/⅔ cup full cream milk
200 g/7 oz/1¾ cups Feta cheese, crumbled
Chopped fresh mint, to garnish

---

① Place the lettuce in a saucepan with the garlic, water, sugar and salt. Cook gently over a low heat until wilted.

② Mix the potato flour to a smooth paste with a little of the milk. Add the remaining milk and stir into the pan.

③ Bring to the boil, stirring all the time. Lower the heat, cover and simmer for 20 minutes.

④ Allow the soup to cool almost completely, then add the Feta.

⑤ Blend in two batches until smooth, then transfer to a bowl, cover and chill.

⑥ Stir before serving sprinkled with a little chopped mint.

PREPARATION TIME: 20 MINUTES
COOKING TIME: 25 MINUTES

Chilled Sweet Soups

*T*he foundation of most of these soups is fruit and I have taken you through the seasons with rhubarb for late spring, berries for summer, currants for autumn (fall) and cranberries for winter. Other soups in this chapter are made using apples, oranges, apricots, pears and melon.

Gooseberry and Rhubarb Soup
SERVES 6

Shades of an English country garden characterise this quaint but delightful soup.

---

225 g/8 oz gooseberries, topped and tailed
175 g/6 oz rhubarb sticks, chopped
600 ml/1 pt/2½ cups water
225 g/8 oz/1 cup caster (superfine) sugar
15 ml/1 tbsp cornflour (cornstarch)
150 ml/¼ pt/⅔ cup apple juice
150 ml/¼ pt/⅔ cup single (light) cream
30 ml/2 tbsp chopped walnuts

---

① Place the gooseberries and rhubarb in a saucepan with the water. Bring to the boil.

② Lower the heat, cover and simmer gently for 20 minutes.

③ Add the sugar and stir until dissolved. Remove from the heat and leave to cool to lukewarm.

④ Blend in two or three batches until smooth, then transfer to a clean saucepan.

⑤ Mix the cornflour to a smooth paste with the apple juice. Add to the soup, then gently bring to the boil and simmer for 1 minute until the soup is slightly thickened.

⑥ Pour into a bowl and place a round of damp greaseproof (waxed) paper directly on top of the soup.

⑦ Leave to cool, then chill for several hours until very cold.

⑧ Before serving, remove the greaseproof paper (any layer of skin will come away with it), stir round and pour into six bowls. Drizzle the cream over each portion and sprinkle with the walnuts.

PREPARATION TIME: 20 MINUTES
COOKING TIME: 25 MINUTES

Mixed Berry Soup
SERVES 6

A star attraction for midsummer.

450 g/1 lb strawberries, hulled
225 g/8 oz raspberries
900 ml/1½ pts/3¾ cups water
1½ large slices of white bread, cubed
150 g/5 oz/⅔ cup caster (superfine) sugar
1 wine glass rosé wine
10 ml/2 tsp cornflour (cornstarch)
15 ml/1 tbsp lemon juice
150 ml/¼ pt/⅔ cup single (light) cream

① Place the strawberries and raspberries in a saucepan with the water and bread. Bring gently to the boil.

② Lower the heat, part-cover and simmer gently for 30 minutes, stirring from time to time.

③ Mix in the sugar and wine and allow cool to lukewarm.

④ Blend in two or three batches until smooth, then transfer to a clean saucepan.

⑤ Mix the cornflour to a smooth paste with the lemon juice. Add to the soup and bring gently to the boil. Lower the heat and simmer for 2 minutes.

⑥ Place a round of damp greaseproof (waxed) paper directly on top of the soup. Leave to cool, then chill for several hours until very cold.

⑦ Before serving, remove the greaseproof paper (any layer of skin will come away with it), stir round and pour into six bowls. Drizzle the cream over each portion.

PREPARATION TIME: 15 MINUTES
COOKING TIME: 35–40 MINUTES

Currant Soup

SERVES 6

*A full-flavoured soup based on two great favourites –
redcurrants or blackcurrants. Crème de cassis (blackcurrant
liqueur) matures the flavours but any rich blackcurrant juice
may be substituted for economy.*

350 g/12 oz fresh red or blackcurrants or a mixture of both
600 ml/1 pt/2½ cups water
15 ml/1 tbsp grated lemon rind
175 g/6 oz/¾ cup caster (superfine) sugar
15 ml/1 tbsp cornflour (cornstarch)
150 ml/¼ pt/⅔ cup crème de cassis
150 ml/¼ pt/⅔ cup single (light) cream
Ground cinnamon, for dusting

① Strip the currants from their stalks and place in a saucepan. Add the water and lemon rind and bring to the boil.

② Lower the heat, cover and simmer gently for 20 minutes.

③ Add the sugar and stir until dissolved. Leave to cool to lukewarm.

④ Blend in two or three batches until smooth, then transfer to a clean saucepan.

⑤ Mix the cornflour to a smooth paste with the crème de cassis. Stir into the pan, then bring gently to the boil and simmer for 1 minute until the soup is slightly thickened.

⑥ Pour into a bowl and place a round of damp greaseproof (waxed) paper directly on top of the soup. Leave to cool, then chill for several hours until very cold.

⑦ Before serving, remove the greaseproof paper (any layer of skin will come away with it), stir round and pour into six bowls. Drizzle the cream over each portion and dust with cinnamon.

PREPARATION TIME: 15 MINUTES
COOKING TIME: 25 MINUTES

Cranberry Soup
SERVES 6

This Scandinavian-inspired soup is slightly sharp and coloured deep winter red. It makes a palate-tingling starter, especially if there's rich poultry or game to follow.

450 g/1 lb fresh or frozen cranberries
750 ml/1¼ pts/3 cups water
15 ml/1 tbsp grated orange rind
275 g/10 oz/1¼ cups caster (superfine) sugar
15 ml/1 tbsp cornflour (cornstarch)
150 ml/¼ pt/⅔ cup red wine
150 ml/¼ pt/⅔ cup single (light) cream
Ground allspice, for dusting

① Place the cranberries in a saucepan with the water and orange rind. Bring to the boil.

② Lower the heat, cover and simmer gently for 20 minutes.

③ Remove from the heat, add the sugar and stir until dissolved. Leave to cool to lukewarm.

④ Blend in two or three batches until smooth, then transfer to a clean saucepan.

⑤ Mix the cornflour to a smooth paste with the wine. Stir into the pan, then bring gently to the boil and simmer for 1 minute until the soup is slightly thickened.

⑥ Pour into a bowl and place a round of damp greaseproof (waxed) paper directly on top of the soup. Leave to cool, then chill for several hours until very cold.

⑦ Before serving, remove the greaseproof paper (any layer of skin will come away with it), stir round and pour into six bowls. Drizzle the cream over each portion and dust with allspice.

PREPARATION TIME: 15 MINUTES
COOKING TIME: 25 MINUTES

Apple and Blackberry Soup
SERVES 6

A much-loved fruit combination, tastefully woven together in this autumnal (fall) soup.

350 g/12 oz cooking (tart) apples, peeled, cored and sliced
225 g/8 oz blackberries
750 ml/1¼ pts/3 cups water
10 ml/2 tsp grated lemon rind
225 g/8 oz/1 cup caster (superfine) sugar
15 ml/1 tbsp cornflour (cornstarch)
150 ml/¼ pt/⅔ cup sweet cider
150 ml/¼ pt/⅔ cup single (light) cream
Ground cinnamon, for dusting

① Place the apples and blackberries in a saucepan with the water and lemon rind. Bring to the boil.

② Lower the heat, cover and simmer gently for 20 minutes.

③ Remove from the heat, add the sugar and stir until dissolved. Leave to cool to lukewarm.

④ Blend in two or three batches until smooth, then transfer to a clean saucepan.

⑤ Mix the cornflour to a smooth paste with the cider. Stir into the pan, then bring gently to the boil and simmer for 1 minute until the soup is slightly thickened.

⑥ Pour into a bowl and place a round of damp greaseproof (waxed) paper directly on top of the soup, Leave to cool, then chill for several hours until very cold.

⑦ Before serving, remove the greaseproof paper (any layer of skin will come away with it), stir round and pour into six bowls. Drizzle the cream over each portion and dust with cinnamon.

PREPARATION TIME: 15 MINUTES
COOKING TIME: 25 MINUTES

Mixed Fruit Soup

SERVES 4

A mellow fruit soup for any occasion.

600 ml/1 pt/2½ cups fresh orange juice
60 ml/4 tbsp caster (superfine) sugar
45 ml/3 tbsp sultanas (golden raisins)
½ ogen melon
1 large orange
1 ripe pear, peeled, cored and chopped
1 eating (dessert) apple, peeled, cored and chopped
15 ml/1 tbsp cornflour (cornstarch)
30 ml/2 tbsp whisky or water

① Place the orange juice, sugar and sultanas in a saucepan. Leave to stand while preparing the fruit.

② Remove the seeds from the melon, then scoop the flesh and juice directly into the saucepan.

③ Peel the orange and cut the flesh into chunks, removing the pips. Add the orange flesh to the pan with the pear and apple.

④ Bring to the boil, then lower the heat. Cover and simmer gently for 40 minutes.

⑤ Leave to cool to lukewarm, then blend in two batches until smooth. Transfer to a clean saucepan.

⑥ Mix the cornflour to a smooth paste with the whisky or water, add to the soup and bring back to the boil. Lower the heat and cook for 1 minute.

⑦ Place a round of damp greaseproof (waxed) paper directly on top of the soup. Leave to cool, then chill for several hours until very cold.

⑧ Before serving, remove the greaseproof paper (any layer of skin will come away with it), stir round and pour into four bowls.

PREPARATION TIME: 30 MINUTES
COOKING TIME: 45–50 MINUTES

Apricot and Cider Soup with Honey
SERVES 6

A mellow and not-too-sweet soup, delicious with ginger snaps or almond biscuits (cookies).

---

250 g/9 oz/1½ cups dried apricots
600 ml/1 pt/2½ cups water
300 ml/½ pt/1¼ cups medium-sweet cider
60 ml/4 tbsp clear honey
45 ml/3 tbsp lemon juice
Juice of 1 lime
1.5 ml/¼ tsp ground allspice

---

① Soak the apricots in water as directed on the packet.

② Drain and transfer to a saucepan with half the water and all the remaining ingredients. Bring gently to the boil.

③ Lower the heat, cover and simmer gently for 40 minutes.

④ Leave to cool to lukewarm, then blend in two batches until smooth.

⑤ Transfer to a large bowl and stir in the remaining water until smooth.

⑥ Cover and chill for several hours until very cold.

⑦ Stir before serving.

PREPARATION TIME: 10 MINUTES, PLUS SOAKING TIME
COOKING TIME: 45 MINUTES

Apricot and Apple Soup
SERVES 8

An attractive, not-too-sweet soup scented with rose water and apricot brandy.

---

200 g/7 oz/generous 1 cup dried apricots
350 g/12 oz cooking (tart) apples, peeled, cored and sliced
600 ml/1 pt/2½ cups freshly pressed apple juice
150 ml/¼ pt/⅔ cup water
15 ml/1 tbsp rose water
30 ml/2 tbsp apricot brandy

---

① Soak the apricots in water as directed on the packet.

② Drain and transfer to a saucepan with the apple slices, apple juice and water. Bring to the boil.

③ Lower the heat, cover and simmer gently for 15 minutes.

④ Leave to cool to lukewarm, then blend in two or three batches until smooth.

⑤ Transfer to a bowl and stir in the rose water and apricot brandy. Cover and chill thoroughly.

⑥ Stir before serving.

PREPARATION TIME: 15 MINUTES, PLUS SOAKING TIME

Soups Using Canned Fruit Fillings

anned fruit fillings – more often used in flans, pies and tarts and on cheesecakes – are an effortless way of making luscious soups at reasonable cost. Most are vividly coloured and can transform a simple meal into a banquet. The origins of fruit soups lie in Central and Northern Europe, where they are served ice-cold as a starter or snack throughout the summer months, often with a topping of milk or cream. Six ideas follow.

Rhubarb and Redcurrant Soup
SERVES 4–5

100 g/4 oz redcurrants
600 ml/1 pt/2½ cups red grape juice
400 g/14 oz/1 large can of rhubarb fruit filling
150 ml/¼ pt/⅔ cup water
60 ml/4 tbsp single (light) cream

① Strip the redcurrants from their stalks and place in the blender with half the grape juice. Blend until smooth.

② Add the fruit filling and blend for 12 seconds.

③ Transfer to a bowl, stir in the remaining grape juice and the water, then cover and chill.

④ Stir before serving with a little cream drizzled over each portion.

PREPARATION TIME: 10 MINUTES

Apple and Perry Soup
SERVES 4

400 g/14 oz/1 large can of apple fruit filling
450 ml/¾ pt/2 cups sparkling perry (pear cider)
15 ml/1 tbsp apricot jam (conserve)
2.5 ml/½ tsp ground cinnamon

① Blend the fruit filling with half the perry, the apricot jam and cinnamon for about 12 seconds until fairly smooth.

② Transfer to a bowl and stir in the remaining perry. Cover and chill.

③ Stir before serving.

PREPARATION TIME: 5 MINUTES

Red Cherry and Raspberry Soup with Cranberry and Rose Water

SERVES 4–5

400 g/14 oz/1 large can of red cherry fruit filling
100 g/4 oz raspberries
600 ml/1 pt/2½ cups cranberry juice
15 ml/1 tbsp rose water

① Blend the fruit filling with the raspberries for about 12 seconds until fairly smooth.

② Transfer to a bowl and stir in the cranberry juice and rose water. Cover and chill.

③ Stir before serving.

PREPARATION TIME: 5 MINUTES

Apricot and Mandarin Orange Soup with Amaretto di Saronno

SERVES 4–5

350 g/12 oz/1 medium can of mandarin oranges in light syrup
400 g/14 oz/1 large can of apricot fruit filling
300 ml/½ pt/1¼ cups water
30 ml/2 tbsp amaretto di saronno

① Blend the contents of the can of mandarin oranges with all the remaining ingredients for about 15 seconds until fairly smooth.

② Cover and chill.

③ Stir before serving.

PREPARATION TIME: 5 MINUTES

Black Cherry and Red Wine Soup
SERVES 4–5

400 g/14 oz/1 large can of black cherry fruit filling
30 ml/2 tbsp sour cherry fruit syrup
300 ml/½ pt/1¼ cups red wine
150 ml/¼ pt/⅔ cup water
5 ml/1 tsp angostura bitters

① Blend the fruit filling, fruit syrup and half the wine for about 15 seconds until fairly smooth. Pour into a bowl.

② Stir in the remaining wine, the water and angostura bitters.

③ Cover and chill.

④ Stir before serving.

PREPARATION TIME: 5 MINUTES

Blackcurrant and Apple Soup
SERVES 4–5

400 g/14 oz/1 large can of blackcurrant fruit filling
600 ml/1 pt/2½ cups apple juice
60 ml/4 tbsp double (heavy) cream

① Blend the fruit filling with half the apple juice for about 10 seconds until fairly smooth.

② Transfer to a bowl and stir in the remaining apple juice. Cover and chill.

③ Stir before serving with a little cream drizzled over each portion.

PREPARATION TIME: 10 MINUTES

Vegetable Soups

*T*his chapter offers the biggest selection of all, featuring every conceivable kind of vegetable – including salad greens – to give you infinite variety and plenty of choice whether for casual eating or more formal dining.

Cauliflower and Cheese Soup
SERVES 4–6

A variation on the cauliflower cheese theme that works well as a soup, you can serve this tasty soup with brown bread and butter or with cream crackers.

225 g/8 oz cauliflower florets
600 ml/1 pt/2½ cups vegetable stock
5 ml/1 tsp salt
15 ml/1 tbsp cornflour (cornstarch)
30 ml/2 tbsp water
300 ml/½ pt/1¼ cups cultured buttermilk
5–10 ml/1–2 tsp made mustard
10 ml/2 tsp lemon juice
100 g/4 oz/1 cup Cheddar cheese, grated
Salt and freshly ground black pepper
30 ml/2 tbsp chopped parsley

1. Place the cauliflower florets in a large pan with the stock and salt. Bring to the boil, then lower the heat and cover the pan. Simmer for about 20–25 minutes until the cauliflower is soft.

2. Remove from the heat and leave to cool to lukewarm.

3. Blend in two batches until smooth, then transfer to a clean saucepan.

4. Mix the cornflour to a smooth paste with the water, then stir into the pan with the buttermilk, mustard and lemon juice.

5. Bring to the boil over a medium–low heat, stirring continuously, then simmer gently for 2 minutes until thickened.

6. Add the cheese and stir gently until melted. Season to taste with salt and pepper.

7. Serve very hot, sprinkled with the parsley.

PREPARATION TIME: 10 MINUTES
COOKING TIME: 30 MINUTES

Broccoli and Stilton Soup with Toasted Almonds

SERVES 4–5

A superior soup, enriched with Stilton cheese and topped with toasted almonds.

25 g/1 oz/¼ cup flaked (slivered) almonds
450 g/1 lb broccoli, cut into pieces
750 ml/1¼ pts/3 cups water
5 ml/1 tsp salt
450 ml/¾ pt/2 cups skimmed milk
5 ml/1 tsp cornflour (cornstarch)
10 ml/2 tsp water
50 g/2 oz/½ cup Stilton cheese, crumbled

1. Toast the almond flakes in a dry frying pan (skillet) over a low heat, turning often. Transfer to a plate and leave to cool.

2. Place the broccoli in a pan with the larger quantity of water and the salt. Bring to the boil.

3. Lower the heat, cover and simmer for 20–25 minutes or until soft. Leave to cool to lukewarm.

4. Blend in two batches until smooth, then transfer to a clean saucepan. Add the milk.

5. Mix the cornflour smoothly with the smaller quantity of water, then stir into the pan.

6. Bring just to the boil, stirring, then simmer gently for 2 minutes.

7. Add the cheese and stir until melted.

8. Serve hot, sprinkling each portion with the toasted almonds.

PREPARATION TIME: 15 MINUTES
COOKING TIME: 30 MINUTES

Mediterranean Summer Vegetable Soup

SERVES 6–8

*This is a distinctive and forceful soup, akin to ratatouille,
seasoned with balsamic vinegar. It is just made for chunks
of rustic brown bread or a baguette and a side dish of
thinly sliced salami.*

15 ml/1 tbsp olive oil
2 onions, thinly sliced
3 garlic cloves, thinly sliced
2 green (bell) peppers, halved and seeded
450 g/1 lb courgettes (zucchini), sliced
450 g/1 lb tomatoes, blanched, skinned and quartered
350 g/12 oz aubergine (eggplant), diced
1.5 litres/2½ pts/6 cups water
5 ml/1 tsp salt
45 ml/3 tbsp balsamic vinegar
30–40 ml/6–8 tsp pesto

① Heat the oil in a large saucepan. Add the onions and garlic and fry (sauté) until golden brown.

② Add the vegetables, water and salt and bring to the boil.

③ Lower the heat, cover and cook gently for 35–40 minutes or until soft. Leave to cool to lukewarm.

④ Blend in three batches until smooth, then transfer to a clean saucepan.

⑤ Reheat until hot and stir in the vinegar.

⑥ Serve in individual bowls, adding 5 ml/1 tsp of pesto to each portion immediately before serving.

PREPARATION TIME: 30 MINUTES
COOKING TIME: 45 MINUTES

Tomato and Mozzarella Soup
SERVES 6

A deep orange soup full of punchy flavours and with a fine consistency.

---

100 g/4 oz/1 cup Mozzarella cheese, cubed
900 ml/1½ pts/3¾ cups tomato juice
15 ml/1 tbsp pesto
30 ml/2 tbsp sun-dried tomato purée (paste)
15 ml/1 tbsp cornflour (cornstarch)
5 ml/1 tsp salt
75 ml/5 tbsp rosé wine
150 ml/¼ pt/⅔ cup water
10–15 ml/2–3 tsp caster (superfine) sugar
Basil leaves, for garnishing

---

① Place the cheese in the blender with half the tomato juice, the pesto, tomato purée, cornflour and salt. Blend until very smooth. Transfer to a large saucepan.

② Mix in the remaining tomato juice with the wine, water and sugar to taste.

③ Cook gently, stirring, over a low heat until the soup comes to the boil and thickens.

④ Simmer for 2 minutes, then serve piping hot garnished with basil leaves.

PREPARATION TIME: 10 MINUTES
COOKING TIME: 10–15 MINUTES

Aubergine Soup with Pine Nuts
SERVES 8

A warming and gently aromatic soup with a full, rich flavour.

---

40 ml/8 tsp pine nuts
30 ml/2 tbsp groundnut (peanut) oil
700 g/1½ lb aubergine (eggplant), unpeeled and cubed
225 g/8 oz onions, chopped
1.5 litres/2½ pts/6 cups water
5–10 ml/1–2 tsp salt
Juice of 1 large lemon
30 ml/2 tbsp tomato purée (paste)

---

① Toast the pine nuts in a dry frying pan (skillet) until lightly golden. Set aside.

② Heat the oil in a large saucepan until sizzling, then add the aubergines and onions.

③ Fry (sauté) gently for 40 minutes, tossing occasionally and keeping the pan covered for the first 20 minutes, then uncovering to evaporate the moisture.

④ Add half the water, the salt, lemon juice and tomato purée. Bring to the boil.

⑤ Lower the heat, cover and simmer gently for 30 minutes. Leave to cool to lukewarm.

⑥ Blend in one or two batches until smooth, then transfer to a clean saucepan.

⑦ Add the remaining water and reheat.

⑧ Serve hot, sprinkling 5 ml/1 tsp of the pine nuts on each serving.

PREPARATION TIME: 30 MINUTES
COOKING TIME: 1¼ HOURS

Mushroom Cappuccino
SERVES 6–8

A delightful foaming mushroom soup. Serve it in cups and saucers with a spoon in the saucer for scooping up the froth.

350 g/12 oz mushrooms
30 ml/2 tbsp melted butter
30 ml/2 tbsp plain (all-purpose) flour
750 ml/1¼ pts/3 cups skimmed milk
5 ml/1 tsp salt, plus a pinch for whipping
1.5 ml/¼ tsp grated nutmeg
2 eggs, separated

① Break up the mushrooms directly into the blender.

② Add the butter, flour and half the milk. Blend to a semi-smooth purée, then transfer to a saucepan.

③ Add the remaining milk, the salt and nutmeg. Heat gently, stirring, until the soup comes to the boil and thickens.

④ Beat the egg yolks into the hot soup, then remove from the heat.

⑤ Whip the egg whites to a stiff snow with a pinch of salt, then whisk evenly into the soup.

⑥ Pour into cups and serve straight away.

PREPARATION TIME: 15 MINUTES
COOKING TIME: 10 MINUTES

Mushroom Soup with Ginger
SERVES 6–7

This flavour combination, though simple, is absolutely striking, making this a rather grand soup for any occasion, at any time of year.

---

150 g/5 oz onions, finely chopped
25 g/1 oz fresh root ginger, finely chopped
25 g/1 oz/2 tbsp butter
7.5 ml/1½ tsp olive oil
1 kg/2¼ lb mushrooms, halved or quartered
1 litre/1¾ pts/4¼ cups hot vegetable stock
150 ml/¼ pt/⅔ cup crème fraîche
30 ml/2 tbsp tomato purée (paste)

---

① Fry (sauté) the onions and ginger gently in the butter and oil in a large saucepan for 7 minutes until pale golden brown.

② Add the mushrooms to the pan and fry for a further 7 minutes, turning frequently.

③ Add the stock and bring to the boil.

④ Lower the heat, cover and simmer for 7 minutes. Leave to cool to lukewarm.

⑤ Blend in two or three batches until smooth, then transfer to a clean saucepan.

⑥ Add the crème fraîche and tomato purée and reheat gently without boiling, stirring from time to time.

⑦ Serve hot.

PREPARATION TIME: 15 MINUTES
COOKING TIME: 25 MINUTES

Russian-style Cabbage Soup
SERVES 6–8

A version of shchi, a popular and economical Russian soup that is a sturdy brew, designed for winter insulation. It is traditionally eaten with dark and heavy rye bread. Blending only half the soup gives it an interesting texture.

---

450 g/1 lb white cabbage, finely shredded
1 large onion, chopped
225 g/8 oz tomatoes, blanched, skinned and chopped
1 litre/1¾ pts/4¼ cups vegetable stock
10 ml/2 tsp salt
150 ml/¼ pt/⅔ cup soured (dairy sour) cream

---

① Place all the ingredients except the soured cream in a saucepan.

② Bring to the boil, stirring from time to time, then cover and simmer gently for 45 minutes. Leave to cool to lukewarm.

③ Transfer only half the soup to a blender and blend until smooth.

④ Return to the pan and reheat until very hot, stirring periodically.

⑤ Serve hot, topping each portion with plenty of soured cream.

PREPARATION TIME: 20 MINUTES
COOKING TIME: 50 MINUTES

Pistou Soup
SERVES 6–8

A speciality from southern France and a relative of minestrone, a condiment called pistou – the locals' name for basil – is stirred into the soup at the last moment,. It is strongly reminiscent of the Italian pesto but without the pine nuts.

For the pistou:
12 basil leaves
175 g/6 oz Parmesan cheese, roughly chopped
4 garlic cloves
60–90 ml/4–6 tbsp olive oil
For the soup:
100 g/4 oz/⅔ cup dried haricot (navy) beans, soaked overnight
2 leeks, halved lengthways
1 onion, coarsely chopped
1 courgette (zucchini), unpeeled and sliced
2 potatoes, peeled and diced
3 tomatoes, coarsely chopped
2 celery stalks, sliced
225 g/8 oz frozen sliced French (green) beans
1.2 litres/2 pts/5 cups water
5–10 ml/1–2 tsp salt
50 g/2 oz cooked macaroni

① To make the pistou, place the basil, Parmesan and garlic in a small blender and, with the machine running, gradually trickle in the olive oil through the hole in the top of the lid to form a creamy leaf-green paste. Set aside.

② To make the soup, drain the haricot beans and place in a saucepan with plenty of cold water.

③ Bring to the boil and keep boiling fairly briskly for 10 minutes, then part-cover and simmer for 40 minutes. Drain and set aside.

④ Place all the vegetables in a large saucepan with half the haricot beans, the measured water and the salt. Bring to the boil, then cover and simmer for 1 hour or until the beans are soft. Leave to cool to lukewarm.

⑤ Blend in two or three batches to a coarse and chunky purée, then transfer to a clean saucepan. Add the remaining haricot beans and the macaroni and reheat until very hot.

⑥ Stir in 30 ml/2 tbsp of the pistou and serve straight away.

Note:
Any leftover pistou can be kept in a screw-topped jar in the refrigerator for up to 3 weeks.

PREPARATION TIME: 15–20 MINUTES FOR THE PISTOU;
30 MINUTES FOR THE SOUP
COOKING TIME: 2–2½ HOURS

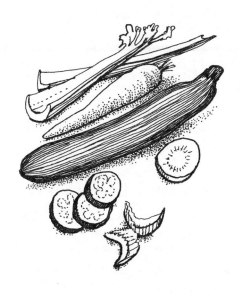

Cream of Turnip Soup

SERVES 4–5

The sweet young turnips used in the soup make it a handsome affair suitable for any occasion.

For the croûtons:
4 large slices of white bread, crusts removed
30–45 ml/2–3 tbsp melted butter or oil
For the soup:
225 g/8 oz turnips, peeled and chopped
225 g/8 oz potatoes, peeled and chopped
175 g/6 oz onions, chopped
1 litre/1¾ pts/4¼ cups water
5 ml/1 tsp salt
150 ml/¼ pt/⅔ cup single (light) cream

---

① To make the croûtons, cut the bread into small cubes and toss in a bowl with the butter or oil.

② Transfer to a large frying pan (skillet) and fry (sauté) over a medium heat, turning occasionally, until golden brown and crispy. Transfer to a plate and leave to cool.

③ To make the soup, place the turnips, potatoes and onions in a saucepan with the water and salt.

④ Bring to the boil, then cover and simmer for about 1 hour or until the vegetables are soft. Leave to cool to lukewarm.

⑤ Blend in two or three batches until very smooth, then transfer to a clean saucepan.

⑥ Add the cream and reheat, stirring, until hot.

⑦ Serve with a sprinkling of the croûtons in each portion.

PREPARATION TIME: 15 MINUTES
COOKING TIME: 1¼ HOURS

Fresh Tomato Soup
SERVES 6

An almost-forgotten splendour amid the vast array of canned varieties. It really is worth making your own.

---

75 g/3 oz lean bacon rashers (slices), chopped
75 g/3 oz carrots, sliced
175 g/6 oz red onions, sliced
1 celery stalk, sliced
20 ml/1½ tbsp sunflower oil
900 g/2 lb ripe tomatoes, blanched, skinned and coarsely chopped
900 ml/1½ pts/3¾ cups vegetable stock
30 ml/2 tbsp tomato purée (paste)
15 ml/1 tbsp brown sugar
5 ml/1 tsp salt
1 bay leaf
15 ml/1 tbsp cornflour (cornstarch)
60 ml/4 tbsp cold water
A little single (light) cream

---

① Gently fry (sauté) the bacon, carrots, onions and celery in the oil in a large saucepan until lightly browned.

② Add the tomatoes, stock, tomato purée, sugar, salt and bay leaf. Bring to the boil, stirring.

③ Lower the heat, cover and simmer for 1 hour. Leave to cool to lukewarm.

④ Remove the bay leaf, then blend in two or three batches until smooth. Transfer to a clean saucepan.

⑤ Mix the cornflour to a smooth paste with the water and add to the pan.

⑥ Bring to the boil and simmer gently for 2 minutes.

⑦ Serve hot, with a little cream trickled over each portion.

PREPARATION TIME: 30 MINUTES
COOKING TIME: 1¼ HOURS

Potato, Carrot and Leek Soup

SERVES 6

An economical and warming soup to make when winter vegetables are in full swing.

---

450 g/1 lb potatoes, peeled and cut into chunks
225 g/8 oz carrots, cut into chunks
3 large leeks, halved lengthways and coarsely sliced
1 litre/1¾ pts/4¼ cups water
5 ml/1 tsp salt
450 ml/¾ pt/2 cups full cream milk
Shredded flatleaf parsley, to garnish

---

① Place the potatoes, carrots and leeks in a saucepan with the water and salt. Bring to the boil.

② Lower the heat, cover and simmer for 50 minutes or until the vegetables are tender. Leave to cool to lukewarm.

③ Blend in two or three batches until smooth, then transfer to a clean saucepan.

④ Stir in the milk, then reheat until hot.

⑤ Garnish each serving with shreds of parsley.

PREPARATION TIME: 20 MINUTES
COOKING TIME: 1 HOUR

Curried Lentil Soup with Carrots
SERVES 6–8

A sustaining soup for all lentil lovers, not just vegetarians.

---

15 ml/1 tbsp sunflower oil
100 g/4 oz onions, thinly sliced
100 g/4 oz carrots, thinly sliced
15 ml/1 tbsp medium-hot curry powder
175 g/6 oz/1 cup red lentils
2.5 ml/½ tsp paprika
1.2 litres/2 pts/5 cups hot water
5 ml/1 tsp salt
2 large slices of brown bread, crumbed
Ground cumin, for dusting

---

① Heat the oil in a saucepan until sizzling. Add the onions and carrots and fry (sauté) for 10 minutes or until lightly golden.

② Stir in the curry powder and cook for 1 minute, stirring all the time.

③ Stir in the lentils, paprika, water and salt. Bring to the boil, stirring.

④ Lower the heat, cover and simmer for 50 minutes, stirring from time to time and adding a little more hot water if the soup seems to be thickening too much. Leave to cool to lukewarm.

⑤ Blend in two batches until smooth, then transfer to a clean saucepan.

⑥ Stir in the breadcrumbs, then reheat until boiling.

⑦ Serve straight away with a dusting of cumin on each portion.

PREPARATION TIME: 15 MINUTES
COOKING TIME: 1¼ HOURS

Marrow and Ginger Soup
SERVES 6

Marrow (squash) and ginger is a tried and trusted combination for jam but it is equally companionable in this gentle, creamy soup with just the merest hint of bite to it.

For the garlic croûtons:
4 large slices of white bread, crusts removed
30–45 ml/2–3 tbsp melted butter or oil
2 garlic cloves, crushed
For the soup:
1.5 kg/3 lb marrow
100 g/4 oz onions, sliced
900 ml/1½ pts/3¾ cups water
15 g/½ oz fresh root ginger, peeled and thinly sliced
5 ml/1 tsp salt
250 g/9 oz German quark

① To make the croûtons, cut the bread into small cubes and toss in a bowl with the butter or oil and the garlic.

② Transfer to a large frying pan (skillet) and fry (sauté) over a medium heat, turning occasionally, until golden brown and crispy. Transfer to a plate and leave to cool.

③ To make the soup, peel and slice the marrow, removing the seeds and fibres. Cut the marrow slices into chunks. Place in a saucepan with the onions, water, ginger and salt.

④ Bring gently to the boil, then lower the heat, cover and simmer gently for 30 minutes or until the vegetables are soft. Leave to cool to lukewarm.

⑤ Stir in the quark, then blend in two or three batches until smooth. Transfer to a clean saucepan and reheat gently without boiling.

⑥ Serve with a topping of the garlic croûtons on each portion.

PREPARATION TIME: 25 MINUTES
COOKING TIME: 40 MINUTES

Yellow Courgette Soup with Onions and Rice Flakes

SERVES 6

A light and mild soup, healthily thickened with brown rice flakes and ideal for vegetarians.

550 g/1¼ lb yellow courgettes (zucchini), thinly sliced
175 g/6 oz onions, coarsely chopped
15 ml/1 tbsp groundnut (peanut) oil
1 litre/1¾ pts/4¼ cups water
5–10 ml/1–2 tsp salt
90 ml/6 tbsp brown rice flakes
150 ml/¼ pt/⅔ cup full cream milk
1.5 ml/¼ tsp grated nutmeg

① Fry (sauté) the courgettes and onions in the oil in a saucepan for about 8 minutes until lightly golden.

② Add the water, salt and rice flakes. Bring gently to the boil, stirring.

③ Lower the heat, cover and simmer for 30 minutes. Leave to cool to lukewarm.

④ Blend in two or three batches to a coarse purée, then transfer to a clean saucepan.

⑤ Stir in the milk and nutmeg and reheat until hot before serving.

PREPARATION TIME: 15 MINUTES
COOKING TIME: 45 MINUTES

Butternut Squash and Peanut Butter Soup

SERVES 6

A rich and succulent, slightly sweet soup, its golden colour stunningly topped with toasted almonds. It sets the right mood for a follow-on stir-fry.

---

45 ml/3 tbsp flaked (slivered) almonds
700 g/1½ lb butternut squash
600 ml/1 pt/2½ cups vegetable stock
60 ml/4 tbsp crunchy peanut butter
250 ml/8 fl oz/1 cup buttermilk
1.5 ml/¼ tsp grated nutmeg
2.5 ml/½ tsp salt

---

① Toast the almond flakes in a dry frying pan (skillet) over a low heat, turning often. Transfer to a plate and leave to cool.

② Halve the squash, leaving in the seeds and place on a microwave plate, cut-sides down. Cook on full power for 15 minutes or until you can easily pierce through the skin and into the flesh with a wooden cocktail stick (toothpick).

③ Leave to cool to lukewarm, then scoop out the seeds and fibres with a spoon and discard. Remove the flesh as close to the skin as possible.

④ Blend with all the remaining ingredients except the almonds until smooth. Transfer to a saucepan and heat until hot but not boiling.

⑤ Sprinkle each portion with the almonds and serve.

PREPARATION TIME: 10 MINUTES
COOKING TIME: 20 MINUTES

Milky Chestnut Soup

SERVES 6

A mild and delicate soup which, despite having only a handful of ingredients, appears lavish and expensive.

450 g/1 lb frozen chestnuts, defrosted
100 g/4 oz onions, sliced
900 ml/1½ pts/3¾ cups skimmed milk
5 ml/1 tsp salt
Ground allspice, for sprinkling

① Place the chestnuts and onions in a saucepan with the milk and salt. Bring gently to the boil.

② Lower the heat, part-cover and simmer gently for 30 minutes. Leave to cool to lukewarm.

③ Blend in two batches until smooth, then transfer to a clean saucepan.

④ Reheat until hot, then serve with a dusting of allspice on each portion.

PREPARATION TIME: 10 MINUTES
COOKING TIME: 40 MINUTES

Cucumber, Pepper and Celery Soup
SERVES 4–5

A lightweight soup with just a touch of butter, making it ideal for slimmers. For the best flavour, make and eat the soup on the same day.

---

225 g/8 oz cucumber, peeled and thinly sliced
100 g/4 oz green (bell) pepper, seeded and cut into strips
3 large celery stalks, chopped
300 ml/½ pt/1¼ cups water
15 ml/1 tbsp cider vinegar
15 ml/1 tbsp cornflour (cornstarch)
2.5 ml/½ tsp mustard powder
2.5 ml/½ tsp salt
300 ml/½ pt/1¼ cups skimmed milk
10 ml/2 tsp butter
30 ml/2 tbsp finely chopped parsley

---

① Place the cucumber, pepper and celery in a blender with the water, vinegar, cornflour, mustard powder and salt. Blend until very smooth.

② Transfer to a saucepan and stir in the milk.

③ Cook, stirring, until the soup comes to the boil and thickens, then simmer for 5 minutes. Stir in the butter.

④ Serve with a sprinkling of parsley on each portion.

PREPARATION TIME: 20 MINUTES
COOKING TIME: 10 MINUTES

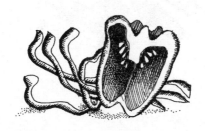

Green Pea Soup

SERVES 6

A vivid fast-track soup with its own unique summer fragrance. A delight!

---

450 g/1 lb frozen peas
1 litre/1¾ pts/4¼ cups vegetable stock
5 ml/1 tsp salt
10 ml/2 tsp cornflour (cornstarch)
15 ml/1 tbsp water
A little single (light) cream

---

① Place the peas in a large saucepan with the stock and salt.

② Mix the cornflour to a smooth paste with the water and pour into the pan. Bring to the boil.

③ Lower the heat and simmer, uncovered, for 3–4 minutes. Leave to cool to lukewarm.

④ Blend in two or three batches until smooth, then transfer to a clean saucepan.

⑤ Reheat before serving with a swirl of cream in each portion.

PREPARATION TIME: 5 MINUTES
COOKING TIME: 7 MINUTES

Green Pea and Lettuce Soup

SERVES 8

This soup is a summer bonus, being attractively coloured,
distinctively flavoured and easy to make.

---

4 little gem lettuces, shredded
450 g/1 lb frozen peas
25 g/1 oz coriander (cilantro) leaves
30 ml/2 tbsp melted butter
5 ml/1 tsp olive oil
1.4 litres/2¼ pts/scant 6 cups water
5 ml/1 tsp salt
150 ml/¼ pt/⅔ cup single (light) cream

---

① Place the lettuces, peas and coriander in a large saucepan.

② Add the butter and oil and toss gently until coated, then add the water and salt.

③ Bring to the boil, then lower the heat, cover and simmer for 20 minutes. Leave to cool to lukewarm.

④ Blend in two or three batches until smooth, then transfer to a clean saucepan. Reheat until very hot.

⑤ Immediately before serving, remove the pan from the heat and stir in the cream.

PREPARATION TIME: 10 MINUTES
COOKING TIME: 25 MINUTES

Artichoke Soup Hollandaise
SERVES 4–5

A high-class soup, delicate and slightly sharp.

400 g/14 oz/1 large can of artichoke hearts
450 ml/¾ pt/2 cups semi-skimmed milk
10 ml/2 tsp plain (all-purpose) flour
2.5 ml/½ tsp salt
15 g/½ oz/1 tbsp butter
2 egg yolks
15 ml/1 tbsp fresh lemon juice

① Place the contents of the can of artichokes in the blender. Add the milk, flour and salt and blend until smooth. Transfer to a saucepan.

② Cook over a low heat, stirring all the time, until the soup comes to the boil and thickens slightly.

③ Add the butter. Simmer for 3 minutes on the lowest possible heat, then remove the pan from the heat and allow the soup to cool slightly.

④ Place a ladleful of soup in a small bowl and mix in the egg yolks and lemon juice (this prevents curdling).

⑤ Tip this mixture back into the pan of soup and stir in gently. Serve straight away.

PREPARATION TIME: 10 MINUTES
COOKING TIME: 10 MINUTES

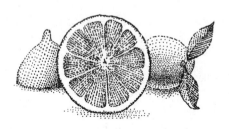

Lentil Soup with Red Onions and Porcini Mushrooms

SERVES 4–5

*Mediterranean in temperament, this soup is dark, sultry,
coarsely textured and a touch smoky. The trace of sweet-sour
in the background comes from the balsamic vinegar.
A marvellous soup to precede French country food or a
rich pasta dish.*

---

350 g/12 oz red onions, coarsely chopped
25 g/1 oz sun-dried (bell) peppers, rinsed and cut into strips
2 garlic cloves (optional), coarsely chopped
175 g/6 oz/1 cup puy lentils, rinsed
1.5 litre/2½ pts/6 cups water
7.5 ml/1½ tsp salt
15 g/½ oz dried porcini mushrooms
50 g/2 oz soft sun-dried tomatoes
60 ml/4 tbsp balsamic vinegar
Freshly grated Parmesan cheese, for sprinkling

---

① Place the onions, peppers and garlic, if using, in a large saucepan with the lentils, water and salt.

② Break pieces of the mushrooms directly into the pan (it is not necessary to soak them first). Bring to the boil.

③ Reduce the heat until the water bubbles noticeably but not vigorously. Continue to cook, uncovered, for 25–30 minutes or until the lentils look fairly swollen and the soup is thick.

④ Blend only half the soup until smooth, then return to the saucepan. Break in the sun-dried tomatoes and add the balsamic vinegar.

⑤ Reheat and serve very hot with a bowl of Parmesan handed separately.

PREPARATION TIME: 15 MINUTES
COOKING TIME: 35 MINUTES

Celery and Leek Soup
SERVES 4–5

*A full-flavoured vegetable soup, lightly spiced with coriander
(cilantro) and laced with crème fraîche.*

---

1 large head of celery, separated into stalks and chopped
2 leeks, halved lengthways and chopped
1 litre/1¾ pts/4¼ cups water
5 ml/1 tsp salt
5 ml/1 tsp ground coriander
150 ml/¼ pt/⅔ cup crème fraîche

---

① Place all the ingredients except the crème fraîche in a large saucepan and bring gently to the boil.

② Lower the heat, cover and simmer for 1 hour or until the vegetables are very soft.

③ Blend in two or three batches until smooth, then transfer to a clean saucepan.

④ Stir in the crème fraîche and reheat gently without boiling.

PREPARATION TIME: 15 MINUTES
COOKING TIME: 1¼ HOURS

Celery and Apple Soup
SERVES 8

*An unexpected mix here: a backdrop of celery, a slight touch
of tartness from the apples, and cream providing extra
smoothness. A winter 'must-make'.*

2 heads of celery
350 g/12 oz onions, coarsely chopped
350 g/12 oz cooking (tart) apples, peeled, cored and
  chopped
1.5 litres/2½ pts/6 cups hot water
5 ml/1 tsp salt
150 ml/¼ pt/⅔ cup whipping cream
45 ml/3 tbsp pistachio nuts, chopped

① Separate the celery into stalks and slice thinly, including the
  leaves.

② Place in a large saucepan with the onions, apples, water
  and salt. Bring to the boil.

③ Lower the heat, cover and simmer gently for 1 hour. Leave
  to cool to lukewarm.

④ Blend in two or three batches until smooth, then transfer to
  a clean saucepan.

⑤ Reheat until hot, then gently whisk in the cream.

⑥ Serve with a sprinkling of nuts on each portion.

PREPARATION TIME: 20 MINUTES
COOKING TIME: 1¼ HOURS

Roasted Yellow Pepper and Yellow Tomato Soup

SERVES 8

*You'll see a flash of sunshine from this warmly coloured soup
with a slightly smoky flavour from the roasted peppers.
Yellow tomatoes may need searching out but they're well
worth the effort, so best make this soup in the summer when
both kinds of vegetable are readily available.*

450 g/1 lb yellow (bell) peppers
1 kg/2¼ lb yellow tomatoes, blanched, skinned and chopped
175 g/6 oz onions, chopped
1.2 litres/2 pts/5 cups water
10 ml/2 tsp caster (superfine) sugar
5–10 ml/1–2 tsp salt
5 ml/1 tsp anchovy essence (extract)
5 ml/1 tsp Worcestershire sauce
To serve:
Garlic croûtons (page 62)

① Grill (broil) the peppers all over, turning frequently with tongs, until the skins blister and char to a dark brown colour. Place in a roomy bowl and cover the top closely with clingfilm (plastic wrap).

② Leave until cold, then rub off the skins under cold running water. Split the peppers and remove the seeds, but save the juices to add to the soup.

③ Place in a large saucepan with all the remaining ingredients and bring to the boil, stirring occasionally.

④ Lower the heat, cover and simmer for 1 hour. Leave to cool to lukewarm.

⑤ Blend in two or three batches, then transfer to a clean saucepan. Reheat until hot and serve with a topping of the garlic croûtons on each portion.

PREPARATION TIME: 35 MINUTES
COOKING TIME: 1¼ HOURS.

Creamed Potato and Herb Soup
SERVES 5–6

A multitude of herbs make their presence felt in this deep green and creamy soup.

---

150 g/5 oz curly parsley
50 g/2 oz flatleaf parsley
50 g/2 oz coriander (cilantro) leaves
8 g/¼ oz basil leaves
450 g/1 lb potatoes, peeled and cubed
600 ml/1 pt/2½ cups skimmed milk
750 ml/1¼ pts/3 cups water
5–10 ml/1–2 tsp salt
150 ml/¼ pt/⅔ cup soured (dairy sour) cream

---

① Place all the herbs in a large bowl of cold water and leave to soak for at least 1 hour, changing the water twice to remove any grit and dust.

② Drain and place in a large saucepan with the potatoes, milk, water and salt. Bring gently to the boil.

③ Lower the heat, cover and simmer for 50 minutes. Leave to cool to lukewarm.

④ Blend in two or three batches until smooth, then transfer to a clean saucepan.

⑤ Add the soured cream and reheat until hot, stirring.

PREPARATION TIME: 10 MINUTES, PLUS SOAKING TIME
COOKING TIME: 1 HOUR

Cucumber and Dill Soup
SERVES 6–8

A mild and attractive soup to make when cucumbers are at their most abundant, generally through the summer months.

---

900 g/2 lb cucumbers, peeled and thinly sliced
30 ml/2 tbsp melted butter
600 ml/1 pt/2½ cups chicken stock
15 ml/1 tbsp cornflour (cornstarch)
450 ml/¾ pt/2 cups full cream milk
7.5 ml/1½ tsp salt
45 ml/3 tbsp chopped dill (dill weed)

---

① Dry the cucumber slices in a clean tea towel (dish cloth), then place in a large saucepan with the butter. Cover and cook over a fairly low heat for 10 minutes.

② Stir in the stock and bring to the boil.

③ Lower the heat, cover and simmer for 20 minutes. Leave to cool to lukewarm.

④ Blend in two or three batches until smooth, then transfer to a clean saucepan.

⑤ Mix the cornflour smoothly with a little of the milk, then add to the soup with the remaining milk and the salt.

⑥ Bring to the boil, stirring, then simmer, uncovered, for 5 minutes.

⑦ Serve with a sprinkling of dill on each portion.

PREPARATION TIME: 10 MINUTES
COOKING TIME: 40 MINUTES

Green Salad Soup

SERVES 6

*Deeply moss green, this soup has a stunning taste and is
ideal for any time of year. It particularly suits a follow-on
omelette or quiche.*

90 g/3½ oz watercress
50 g/2 oz rocket leaves
90 g/3½ oz small spinach leaves
40 g/1½ oz flatleaf parsley
12 shallots, peeled but left whole
15 ml/1 tbsp groundnut (peanut) oil
225 g/8 oz potatoes, peeled and cubed
1.2 litres/2 pts/5 cups vegetable stock
7.5 ml/1½ tsp salt

① Place the watercress, rocket, spinach and parsley in a large bowl of cold water and leave to soak for at least 30 minutes, changing the water twice to remove any grit and dust.

② Fry (sauté) the shallots in the oil in a large saucepan for about 7 minutes, turning frequently, until golden brown.

③ Drain the salad leaves and add to the pan with the potatoes, stock and salt. Bring to the boil.

④ Lower the heat, cover and simmer for 30 minutes. Leave to cool to lukewarm.

⑤ Blend in two or three batches until smooth, then transfer to a clean saucepan.

⑥ Reheat until very hot before serving.

PREPARATION TIME: 15 MINUTES, PLUS SOAKING TIME
COOKING TIME: 50 MINUTES

Meat Soups

A fairly substantial group of soups, featuring all varieties of meat including Parma ham or bacon with celeriac (celery root) and carrots, lamb with aubergine (eggplant), ham and split peas, chicken with a Middle Eastern flavour, turkey and root vegetables, soups from Asia, game soup with wine, old-fashioned mulligatawny and even corned beef with potato.

Celeriac Soup with Parma Ham
SERVES 8

A strong and compelling blend of flavours underpins this comforting winter soup.

---

450 g/l lb celeriac (celery root), diced
225 g/8 oz carrots, diced
3 medium leeks, halved lengthways and sliced
2 litres/3½ pts/8½ cups water
5–10 ml/1–2 tsp salt
15 ml/1 tbsp vegetable stock powder
45 ml/3 tbsp Dijon mustard
60 ml/4 tbsp chopped coriander (cilantro)
100 g/4 oz Parma ham, cut into shreds

---

① Place all the ingredients except half the coriander and the Parma ham in a large saucepan and bring to the boil.

② Lower the heat, cover and simmer gently for 35 minutes or until the vegetables are soft. Leave to cool to lukewarm.

③ Blend in two or three batches until smooth, then transfer to a clean saucepan.

④ Bring gently back to the boil, then serve piping hot, sprinkling each portion with the remaining coriander and the Parma ham shreds.

PREPARATION TIME: 25 MINUTES
COOKING TIME: 45 MINUTES

Celeriac, Onion and Potato Soup with Crispy Bacon

SERVES 8

Almost a meal in itself, this is an energy-giving and fulfilling family soup.

225 g/8 oz onions, sliced
30 ml/2 tbsp groundnut (peanut) oil
550 g/1¼ lb potatoes, peeled and cubed
550 g/1¼ lb celeriac (celery root), peeled and cubed
1.5 litres/2½ pts/6 cups water
5 ml/1 tsp salt
1.5 ml/¼ tsp grated nutmeg
200 g/7 oz streaky bacon, snipped crossways into strips
45 ml/3 tbsp chopped parsley

① Fry (sauté) the onions gently in the oil in a large saucepan for about 10 minutes until lightly golden.

② Add the potatoes, celeriac, water, salt and nutmeg. Bring to the boil.

③ Lower the heat, cover and simmer gently for 1¼ hours or until the vegetables are soft. Leave to cool to lukewarm.

④ Blend in two or three batches to a coarse purée, then transfer to a clean saucepan.

⑤ Fry the bacon in its own fat until very crispy.

⑥ Reheat the soup until hot and serve with the bacon and parsley scattered over each portion.

PREPARATION TIME: 35 MINUTES
COOKING TIME: 1¾ HOURS

Lamb and Aubergine Soup
SERVES 6

A tasty soup, slightly Middle Eastern in character. Eat with warm pitta bread for a substantial first course.

350 g/12 oz minced (ground) lamb
1 large leek, halved lengthways and sliced
450 g/1 lb aubergine (eggplant), unpeeled and cubed
2 garlic cloves, sliced
900 ml/1½ pts/3¾ cups beef stock
5 ml/1 tsp salt
15 ml/1 tbsp malt vinegar
5 ml/1 tsp cornflour (cornstarch)
2.5 ml/½ tsp ground cinnamon
30 ml/2 tbsp lemon juice
45 ml/3 tbsp plain yoghurt

① Dry-fry (sauté) the lamb in a heavy-based saucepan for about 7 minutes, stirring frequently, until the grains are browned and separated.

② Add the leek, aubergine and garlic and fry, turning frequently, until the vegetables begin to brown.

③ Add the stock and salt and bring gently to the boil, stirring occasionally.

④ Mix together the vinegar and cornflour, then add to the soup with the cinnamon and lemon juice. Return to the boil, stirring.

⑤ Lower the heat, cover and simmer gently for 40 minutes. Leave to cool to lukewarm.

⑥ Blend in batches until smooth. Cover and chill overnight.

⑦ Remove any hard layer of fat from the top, then transfer the soup to a saucepan and reheat until just boiling. Serve straight away, topping each portion with a spoonful of yoghurt.

PREPARATION TIME: 30 MINUTES
COOKING TIME: 1 HOUR, PLUS REHEATING

Avocado and Asparagus Beef Soup
SERVES 4

An earthy soup with a creamy texture, wonderful with a dark brown bread.

---

1 large ripe avocado, halved and stoned (pitted)
300 g/11 oz/1 medium can of condensed beef consommé
375 g/13 oz/1 large jar of green asparagus
600 ml/1 pt/2½ cups water
5 ml/1 tsp salt
150 ml/¼ pt/⅔ cup plain yoghurt
4 slices of lemon

---

① Scoop the avocado flesh into the blender and add the consommé, the contents of the jar of asparagus, half the water and the salt.

② Blend until smooth, then transfer to a saucepan and gently whisk in the remaining water. Bring just to the boil, stirring.

③ Thoroughly stir in the yoghurt, then spoon into bowls, topping each one with a slice of lemon. Serve straight away.

PREPARATION TIME: 5 MINUTES
COOKING TIME: 5 MINUTES

Yellow Split Pea Soup with Ham
SERVES 6

A rustic soup and a European winter classic from as far afield as Scandinavia to Turkey.

---

225 g/8 oz/1⅓ cups yellow split peas, soaked overnight
1 large ham bone
175 g/6 oz parsnips, sliced
100 g/4 oz carrots, sliced
100 g/4 oz onions, sliced
175 g/6 oz potatoes, peeled and sliced
1.5 litres/2½ pts/6 cups water
1 bay leaf
5–10 ml/1–2 tsp salt
45 ml/3 tbsp chopped parsley

---

① Drain the split peas and place in a saucepan with the remaining ingredients except the parsley.

② Bring to the boil and boil briskly for 10 minutes.

③ Lower the heat, part-cover and simmer for 1–1½ hours or until the split peas are tender. Leave to cool to lukewarm.

④ Remove and discard the ham bone and bay leaf, picking any remaining meat off the bone and returning it to the saucepan.

⑤ Blend in two or three batches to a semi-smooth purée, then transfer to a clean saucepan.

⑥ Reheat until very hot and serve with the parsley sprinkled on each portion.

PREPARATION TIME: 20 MINUTES
COOKING TIME: 1¼–1¾ HOURS

Middle Eastern Chicken and Vegetable Soup

SERVES 8

A sturdy soup that puts chicken wings to great use.

175 g/6 oz carrots, cubed
225 g/8 oz potatoes, peeled and cubed
175 g/6 oz parsnips, cubed
225 g/8 oz onions, sliced
1 celery stalk, sliced
225 g/8 oz marrow (squash) or pumpkin
  (prepared weight)
1.75 litres/3 pts/7½ cups chicken stock
60 ml/4 tbsp barley
30 ml/2 tbsp porridge oats
5 ml/1 tsp salt
8 chicken wings

① Place all the ingredients except the chicken wings in a large saucepan and bring to the boil.

② Lower the heat, cover and simmer gently for 45 minutes.

③ Add the chicken wings and continue to cook for a further 25 minutes or until the vegetables are soft.

④ Remove the wings and set aside. Leave the soup to cool to lukewarm.

⑤ Blend in two or three batches to a coarse purée, then transfer to a clean saucepan.

⑥ Return the wings to the soup and reheat gently, stirring from time to time, until very hot.

⑦ Serve straight away, making sure each portion has a chicken wing.

PREPARATION TIME: 25 MINUTES
COOKING TIME: 1¼ HOURS

Swiss-style Green Onion Soup
SERVES 6

Called green because of its lavish garnish of chives, this soup is light, tasty and attractive to look at – a useful starter at any time of year.

450 g/1 lb onions, sliced
60 ml/4 tbsp melted butter
5 ml/1 tsp olive oil
20 ml/4 tsp plain (all-purpose) flour
900 ml/1½ pts/3¾ cups hot chicken or beef stock
5 ml/1 tsp salt
150 ml/¼ pt/⅔ cup whipping cream
90 ml/6 tbsp snipped fresh chives

① Place the onions in a saucepan with the butter and oil. Part-cover and fry (sauté) very gently for about 20 minutes until the onions begin to soften but do not allow to brown.

② Stir in the flour and cook for 1 minute, then gradually work in the stock. Add the salt and bring gently to the boil, stirring.

③ Lower the heat, cover and simmer gently for 25 minutes, stirring from time to time. Leave to cool to lukewarm.

④ Blend in two or three batches until smooth, then transfer to a clean saucepan.

⑤ Gently whisk in the cream and reheat until hot without boiling.

⑥ Serve straight away, with a sprinkling of chives on each portion.

PREPARATION TIME: 20 MINUTES
COOKING TIME: 50 MINUTES

Turkey Soup with Lemon and Thyme
SERVES 6–8

After every Christmas dinner, one is confronted with yet another turkey carcass, a poignant reminder of the holiday festivities. Don't let it go to waste – try this bright and cheery soup that makes an appetising main-meal filler with a plate of brown bread sandwiches and some coleslaw.

100 g/4 oz carrots, cut into chunks
100 g/4 oz potatoes, cut into chunks
100 g/4 oz swede (rutabaga) or parsnip, cut into chunks
175 g/6 oz onions, cut into chunks
1 large leek, sliced
45 ml/3 tbsp brown rice
1 turkey carcass, broken into pieces
1.75 litres/3 pts/7½ cups water
15 ml/1 tbsp chopped tarragon
2 whole garlic cloves
10 ml/2 tsp finely grated lemon rind
5 ml/1 tsp dried thyme
5 ml/1 tsp salt
45–60 ml/3–4 tbsp melted butter

① Place all the ingredients except the melted butter in a large saucepan. Bring gently to the boil.

② Lower the heat, cover and simmer gently for 1¼ hours.

③ Remove the carcass, take off any pieces of meat and stuffing still remaining and return to the pan. Discard the bones. Leave the soup to cool to lukewarm.

④ Blend in three or four batches until semi-smooth, then transfer to a clean saucepan.

⑤ Reheat until very hot, then serve with a drizzle of melted butter on each portion.

PREPARATION TIME: 30 MINUTES
COOKING TIME: 1½ HOURS

Chicken Broth with Barley and Sage
SERVES 6–8

This country-style soup, packed with vegetables and thickened with barley, is a practical way to put a chicken carcass to good use.

1 chicken carcass, broken into pieces
1.5 litres/2½ pts/6 cups beef stock
40 g/1½ oz barley
2 celery sticks, sliced
1 leek, halved lengthways and sliced
225 g/8 oz carrots, sliced
225 g/8 oz cauliflower florets
1.5 ml/¼ tsp dried sage
5 ml/1 tsp salt
30–45 ml/2–3 tbsp dried fried (sautéed) onions

① Place the carcass in a large saucepan with the stock and barley. Bring gently to the boil.

② Add the remaining ingredients except the dried onions, mix well and return to the boil.

③ Lower the heat, cover and simmer gently for 1¼ hours.

④ Remove the carcass, take off any pieces of meat and stuffing still remaining and return to the pan. Discard the bones. Leave the soup to cool to lukewarm.

⑤ Blend in three or four batches until semi-smooth, then transfer to a clean saucepan.

⑥ Reheat the soup until very hot and serve with a sprinkling of the dried onions on each portion.

PREPARATION TIME: 30 MINUTES
COOKING TIME: 1½ HOURS

Chicken Soup with Fennel and Tapioca
SERVES 4–5

A well-seasoned and colourful soup, the fennel adding a subtle hint of anise and the tapioca performing brilliantly as an unobtrusive thickener.

45 ml/3 tbsp tapioca
1 leg and thigh chicken joint, about 225 g/8 oz
175 g/6 oz onions, coarsely chopped
2 celery stalks, sliced
1 head of fennel, about 225 g/8 oz, sliced
15 g/½ oz parsley
900 ml/1½ pts/3¾ cups water
300 ml/½ pt/1¼ cups carrot juice
5 ml/1 tsp salt

① Soak the tapioca in enough water to cover for a minimum of 1 hour.

② Place the remaining ingredients in a large saucepan and bring to the boil, stirring.

③ Lower the heat, cover and simmer gently for 1 hour.

④ Remove the chicken joint and leave the soup to cool to lukewarm.

⑤ Take the meat off the chicken joint and shred with two forks. Set aside.

⑥ Blend the soup in two or three batches to a coarse purée, then transfer to a clean saucepan.

⑦ Add the tapioca and soaking water to the pan and bring to the boil. Lower the heat, add the chicken shreds and simmer for 10 minutes.

⑧ Serve very hot.

PREPARATION TIME: 15 MINUTES, PLUS SOAKING TIME
COOKING TIME: 1¼ HOURS

Asian Chicken Soup with Basmati Rice and Lentils

SERVES 4–5

A powerfully seasoned and spicy soup, lightened with a dash of yoghurt.

1 leg and thigh chicken joint, about 225 g/8 oz
175 g/6 oz onions, coarsely chopped
1 green chilli, slit and seeds removed
2–3 garlic cloves, thinly sliced
25 g/1 oz fresh root ginger, thinly sliced
25 g/1 oz coriander (cilantro) leaves
10 ml/2 tsp garam masala
5 ml/1 tsp ground cumin
2.5 ml/½ tsp ground turmeric
2.5 ml/½ tsp ground coriander
45 ml/3 tbsp orange lentils
30 ml/2 tbsp basmati rice
5–7.5 ml/1–1½ tsp salt
1.2 litres/2 pts/5 cups water
150 ml/¼ pt/⅔ cup plain yoghurt
To serve:
Naan breads

① Place the chicken, onions, chilli, garlic, ginger and coriander leaves in a large saucepan.

② Sprinkle the garam masala, cumin, turmeric and ground coriander over the chicken and vegetables, then mix in the lentils and rice.

③ Add the salt and water and bring to the boil, stirring.

④ Lower the heat, cover and simmer gently for 1 hour.

⑤ Remove the chicken joint and leave the soup to cool to lukewarm. Take the meat off the chicken joint and cut into strips. Set aside.

⑥ Blend the soup in two or three batches to a coarse purée, then transfer to a clean saucepan. Bring to the boil, stirring.

⑦ Add the chicken strips and simmer for 10 minutes.

⑧ Stir in the yoghurt and serve very hot with naan breads.

PREPARATION TIME: 30 MINUTES
COOKING TIME: 1¾ HOURS

Couscous and Cabbage Soup with Sausages
SERVES 5–6

A meal of a soup, thickened with couscous and well seasoned. For speed, you can use shredded frozen cabbage.

450 g/1 lb green cabbage, shredded
45 ml/3 tbsp couscous
1.5 litres/2½ pts/6 cups water
5 ml/1 tsp wholegrain mustard
1.5 ml/¼ tsp ground allspice
5 ml/1 tsp salt
450 g/1 lb cooked pork sausages, diagonally sliced

① Place all the ingredients except the sausages in a large saucepan. Bring to the boil.

② Lower the heat, cover and simmer for 40 minutes, stirring occasionally. Leave to cool to lukewarm.

③ Blend in two or three batches to a coarse purée, then transfer to a clean saucepan.

④ Add the sausage slices and reheat until very hot.

PREPARATION TIME: 10 MINUTES
COOKING TIME: 50 MINUTES

Tandoori Lamb Soup
SERVES 6

A deep orange soup with Indian spices, a beauty topped with thick yoghurt and shredded cucumber.

20 ml/4 tsp groundnut (peanut) oil
175 g/6 oz onions, coarsely chopped
2 garlic cloves, thinly sliced
1 red (bell) pepper, seeded and coarsely chopped
100 g/4 oz fresh spinach leaves, torn into small pieces
225 g/8 oz minced (ground) lamb
30 ml/2 tbsp tandoori spice mix
5 ml/1 tsp ground cardamom
2.5 ml/½ tsp ground ginger
1.5 ml/¼ tsp ground allspice
30 ml/2 tbsp chutney
45 ml/3 tbsp chopped coriander (cilantro)
30 ml/2 tbsp tomato purée (paste)
1.5 litres/2½ pts/6 cups water
5–10 ml/1–2 tsp salt
30 ml/2 tbsp plain yoghurt
30 ml/2 tbsp shredded cucumber

① Heat the oil in a large saucepan until sizzling.

② Add the onions, garlic, chopped pepper and spinach and fry (sauté) gently for 10 minutes or until the vegetables are just beginning to turn golden.

③ Mix in the lamb and cook, stirring often, until the grains of lamb are browned and separated. Continue cooking for a further 10 minutes.

④ Add all the spices, then the chutney, coriander, tomato purée, water and salt. Bring to the boil, stirring.

⑤ Lower the heat, cover and simmer gently for 1 hour, stirring occasionally. Leave to cool, then chill for about 12 hours.

⑥ Remove any hard layer of fat from the surface, then blend the soup in two or three batches to a coarse purée.

⑦ Transfer to a clean saucepan and reheat until very hot.

⑧ Serve each portion topped with the yoghurt and cucumber.

PREPARATION TIME: 30 MINUTES
COOKING TIME: 1½ HOURS

Imperial Chinese Chicken Soup

SERVES 4–5

An Anglo-Chinese broth, thickened with red rice and spiced in the Far Eastern tradition.

---

350 g/12 oz onions, coarsely chopped
25 g/1 oz fresh root ginger, coarsely chopped
2 celery stalks, sliced
225 g/8 oz boned chicken breast
30 ml/2 tbsp low-salt soy sauce
15 ml/1 tbsp mushroom ketchup (catsup)
5 ml/1 tsp five-spice powder
45 ml/3 tbsp red imperial rice
1.2 litres/2 pts/5 cups water
5 ml/1 tsp salt
30 ml/2 tbsp lemon juice
5–20 ml/1–4 tsp chilli sauce
100 g/4 oz/2 cups beansprouts

---

① Place all the ingredients except the lemon juice, chilli sauce and beansprouts in a large saucepan. Bring to the boil, stirring.

② Lower the heat, cover and simmer gently for 1 hour.

③ Remove the chicken breast and leave the soup to cool to lukewarm. Cut the meat into small cubes.

④ Blend the soup in two or three batches to a coarse purée, then transfer to a clean saucepan.

⑤ Add the lemon juice and chilli sauce to taste and bring to the boil. Lower the heat and simmer for 5 minutes.

⑥ Add the chicken cubes and beansprouts and reheat for 5 minutes.

⑦ Serve very hot.

PREPARATION TIME: 25 MINUTES
COOKING TIME: 1½ HOURS

Kidney Soup
SERVES 4

A sophisticated classic from yesteryear.

250 g/9 oz lambs' kidneys
175 g/6 oz onions, thinly sliced
15 ml/1 tbsp groundnut (peanut) oil
600 ml/1 pt/2½ cups water
5 ml/1 tsp salt
15 ml/1 tbsp plain (all-purpose) flour
450 ml/¾ pt/2 cups dry red wine
15 ml/1 tbsp redcurrant jelly (clear conserve)
10 ml/2 tsp Worcestershire sauce
4 ml/¾ tsp made English mustard
To serve:
Cheese straws or biscuits (crackers)

① Wash and slice the kidneys, removing excess fat from the centre of each slice.

② Gently fry (sauté) the onions in the oil in a saucepan for about 12 minutes until a warm golden brown.

③ Add the kidneys and fry for 10 minutes.

④ Add the water and salt and bring gently to the boil.

⑤ Lower the heat, cover and simmer gently for 40 minutes, stirring occasionally. Leave to cool to lukewarm. Add the flour.

⑥ Blend until fairly smooth and return to the saucepan. Add the wine, redcurrant jelly, Worcestershire sauce and mustard.

⑦ Cook, stirring, until the soup comes to the boil and thickens. Simmer for 5 minutes.

⑧ Serve each portion accompanied by a cheese straw or biscuit.

PREPARATION TIME: 25 MINUTES
COOKING TIME: 1¼ HOURS

Game Soup with Wine, Cream and Orange

SERVES 8

A classy venison soup tastefully seasoned with juniper berries.

30 ml/2 tbsp sunflower oil
100 g/4 oz onions, cut into small cubes
100 g/4 oz carrots, cut into small cubes
225 g/8 oz potatoes, peeled and cut into small cubes
175 g/6 oz venison steak
225 g/8 oz tomatoes, blanched, skinned and coarsely chopped
750 ml/1¼ pts/3 cups beef stock
300 ml/½ pt/1¼ cups red wine
15 ml/1 tbsp tomato purée (paste)
10 ml/2 tsp brown sugar
10 ml/2 tsp lemon juice
6 juniper berries, crushed
5 ml/1 tsp salt
150 ml/¼ pt/⅔ cup single (light) cream
Finely grated orange rind, to garnish

① Heat the oil in a large saucepan until sizzling.

② Add the onions, carrots and potatoes and fry (sauté) gently, part-covered, for 10 minutes.

③ Add the venison and fry for 6 minutes, turning twice.

④ Add the tomatoes and fry for 5 minutes.

⑤ Thoroughly mix in the stock, wine, tomato purée, sugar, lemon juice, juniper berries and salt. Bring gently to the boil.

⑥ Lower the heat, cover and simmer for 45 minutes or until the vegetables are tender.

⑦ Lift out the venison and cut into narrow strips. Leave the soup to cool to lukewarm.

⑧ Blend the soup in two or three batches until smooth, then transfer to a clean saucepan.

⑨ Add the venison and reheat the soup until very hot. Stir in the cream.

⑩ Serve with a sprinkling of orange rind on each portion.

PREPARATION TIME: 40 MINUTES
COOKING TIME: 1¼ HOURS

Butter Bean Soup

SERVES 6

Based on an old South African recipe, this soup is a much-loved winter standby and is appreciated for its sustaining qualities. The rapid boiling at step 1 is necessary to destroy the toxins in the dried beans.

---

225 g/8 oz/1⅓ cups dried butter (lima) beans, soaked overnight
1.5 litres/2½ pts/6 cups beef stock
175 g/6 oz onions, cubed
350 g/12 oz potatoes, peeled and cubed
175 g/6 oz tomatoes, blanched, skinned and coarsely chopped
2 back bacon rashers (slices), trimmed and cut into strips
5 ml/1 tsp chopped parsley

---

① Drain the beans and place in a large saucepan with the stock. Bring to the boil and boil briskly for 10 minutes.

② Add the onions, potatoes, tomatoes and bacon and return to the boil.

③ Lower the heat, cover and simmer for 1 hour. Leave to cool to lukewarm.

④ Blend in two or three batches to a coarse purée, then transfer to a clean saucepan.

⑤ Before serving, reheat the soup to piping hot and sprinkle each portion with the parsley.

PREPARATION TIME: 20 MINUTES
COOKING TIME: 1¼ HOURS

Mulligatawny Soup
SERVES 6

An old Anglo-Indian friend from the days of the British Raj.

30 ml/2 tbsp groundnut (peanut) oil
175 g/6 oz carrots, sliced
175 g/6 oz onions, sliced
2 celery stalks, cut into short lengths
25 g/1 oz/¼ cup plain (all purpose) flour
15 ml/1 tbsp Madras curry powder
1 litre/1¾ pts/4¼ cups hot beef stock
175 g/6 oz cooking (tart) apples, peeled, cored and
  coarsely chopped
30 ml/2 tbsp raisins
30 ml/2 tbsp lemon juice
10 ml/2 tsp brown sugar
5 ml/1 tsp salt
75 g/3 oz/¾ cup cooked chicken, cut into narrow strips
90 g/3½ oz/7 tbsp cooked rice
45 ml/3 tbsp plain yoghurt

① Heat the oil in a large saucepan until sizzling. Add the carrots, onions and celery and fry (sauté) until lightly golden. Stir in the flour and curry powder and cook for 2 minutes.

② Blend in the hot stock a little at a time, then cook, stirring, until the mixture comes to the boil and thickens.

③ Add the apples, raisins, lemon juice, sugar and salt and return to the boil. Lower the heat, cover and simmer gently for 1 hour, stirring fairly often to prevent sticking. Leave to cool to lukewarm.

④ Blend in two or three batches until smooth, then transfer to a clean saucepan. Reheat gently until hot.

⑤ Divide the chicken strips and rice equally between warm soup bowls and top up with hot soup. Add a spoonful of yoghurt to each and serve.

PREPARATION TIME: 30 MINUTES
COOKING TIME: 1¼ HOURS

Corned Beef and Potato Soup
SERVES 4–6

A thick and filling family soup, simple and quick for busy cooks to make.

---

340 g/12 oz/1 medium can of corned beef
545 g/1¼ lb/1 very large can of potatoes in water or brine
600 ml/1 pt/2½ cups water
10 ml/2 tsp made English mustard
5 ml/1 tsp salt
30 ml/2 tbsp brown ketchup (catsup)
90 ml/6 tbsp chopped parsley

---

① Halve the block of corned beef. Coarsely mash one half and cut the other into small pieces.

② Drain the potatoes, reserving the liquid. Cut the potatoes into small pieces.

③ Place in the blender with the reserved liquid and half the water. Blend until fairly smooth and pour into a saucepan.

④ Stir in the remaining water, the mashed corned beef, the mustard, salt and ketchup. Bring to the boil, stirring all the time.

⑤ Lower the heat and simmer for 5 minutes.

⑥ Add the remaining corned beef and mix in thoroughly.

⑦ Serve very hot and shower each portion heavily with the parsley.

PREPARATION TIME: 10 MINUTES
COOKING TIME: 10 MINUTES

Fish Soups

*B*ecause fish soup is less familiar in Britain than in its European neighbours and other countries even further afield, the selection in this chapter has been narrowed down to speciality soups with gourmet appeal from the Far East and France.

Penang Laksa
SERVES 6

More a soupy fish meal than just a soup, laksa is a fish stock with seasonings and coconut milk, afloat with rice vermicelli, seafood, vegetables and sometimes fruit. A Malaysian speciality – with no two versions alike – it is sold by street hawkers in the Far East and also made at home by dedicated cooks. Its preparation is long but the end result is a joyful and memorable eating experience. It is a dramatic favourite with the 'smart set' from India to Thailand to China, brilliant for entertaining if you only want a one-dish meal.
Start with the additions, which can be made early on and left, covered and chilled, until the laksa is ready to be served.

Additions:
1 small lettuce, shredded
¼ cucumber, unpeeled and diced
6 spring onions (scallions), thinly sliced
10 mint leaves, cut into strips
A 2.5 cm/1 in slice of fresh pineapple, cut into small pieces
90 ml/6 tbsp beansprouts
400 g/14 oz frozen king prawns (jumbo shrimp),
   defrosted as directed on the packet
For the laksa:
2 stalks of lemon grass, cut into short lengths
2 garlic cloves, halved
A walnut-sized piece of fresh root ginger, sliced
1 onion, sliced
8 macadamia nuts or blanched almonds
2 large sun-dried red chillies
30 ml/2 tbsp chopped coriander (cilantro)
5 ml/1 tsp ground turmeric
15 ml/1 tbsp fish sauce
400 ml/14 fl oz/1¾ cups canned coconut milk
5 ml/1 tsp salt
1.2 litres/2 pts/5 cups well-flavoured fish stock
250 g/9 oz rice vermicelli

① Arrange the additions attractively on a large plate, keeping each one separate. Cover with clingfilm (plastic wrap) and chill until ready to serve.

② To make the laksa, place the lemon grass, garlic, ginger, onion, nuts, chillies, a quarter of the coriander, the turmeric, fish sauce, coconut milk and salt in a blender and blend until smooth.

③ Transfer to a large saucepan and add the fish stock. Bring to the boil.

④ Meanwhile, soak the vermicelli in boiling water for 5 minutes. Drain and divide between six large, deep soup bowls. Sprinkle with the prawns and other additions, then top up with the boiling stock.

⑤ Sprinkle heavily with the remaining coriander and serve straight away.

Notes:

① For convenience, you could substitute fish stock cubes and water for the fish stock and canned pineapple for fresh.

② As a variation, use cooked and flaked salmon or salmon trout, or any other cooked and flaked white fish, instead of the prawns.

③ For a hotter soup, increase the chillies to a maximum of eight.

PREPARATION TIME: 1–1¼ HOURS
COOKING TIME: 15 MINUTES

Classic Fish Soup
SERVES 8

*The star attraction of the show and a glittering performer, this
is soup at its very finest: a soft and smooth blend of assorted
fish and vegetables simmered in fish stock with saffron to give
a note of exclusivity. Particular to the South of France, the
soup has been lovingly developed over many years by the
international restaurant fraternity and, should you be eating
out and order a fish soup, there is a strong possibility that it
will closely resemble the one given here. Rouille, a traditional
and fairly fiery condiment, is stirred into each portion at the
table to further enrich and enliven the flavour.*

For the soup:
1.5–2.5 ml/¼–½ tsp saffron strands
15 ml/1 tbsp hot water
250 g/9 oz onions, very thinly sliced
2 garlic cloves, very thinly sliced
1 celery stick, very thinly sliced
25 ml/1½ tbsp olive or groundnut (peanut) oil
450 g/1 lb tomatoes, blanched, skinned and coarsely
  chopped
30 ml/2 tbsp tomato purée (paste)
350 g/12 oz hake or haddock fillet, skinned and cubed
450 g/1 lb salmon fillet, skinned and cubed
1.5 litres/2½ pts/6 cups cold water
300 ml/½ pt/1¼ cups dry white wine
5 ml/1 tsp salt
For the rouille:
75 g/3 oz bread slices with crusts, cubed
1 red chilli, about 50 g/2 oz, halved and seeded
3 garlic cloves
30 ml/2 tbsp tomato purée (paste)
45 ml/3 tbsp olive oil
30 ml/2 tbsp boiling water
2.5 ml/½ tsp salt
To serve:
Baguette slices

① To make the soup, soak the saffron in the hot water in a small basin for a minimum of 30 minutes.

② Place the onions, garlic and celery in a saucepan with the oil and fry (sauté) for 5–6 minutes until they are just beginning to turn lightly golden.

③ Add the remaining ingredients, including the saffron and soaking water. Bring to the boil,

④ Lower the heat, cover and simmer gently for 45 minutes, stirring once or twice. Leave to cool to lukewarm.

⑤ To make the rouille, place all the ingredients in the blender and blend to form a smooth paste.

⑥ Blend the soup in two or three batches until smooth, then transfer to a clean saucepan.

⑦ Reheat until very hot before serving with a side dish of rouille and slices of baguette.

Notes:

① An easier rouille can be made by mixing 90 ml/6 tbsp thick mayonnaise with 2 peeled and crushed garlic cloves and 30 ml/2 tbsp chilli sauce.

② After blending, the rouille can be packed into a screw-topped jar, the top smoothed and then coated with extra oil, and stored for up to 10 days. Stir before serving.

PREPARATION TIME: 40 MINUTES FOR THE SOUP, PLUS SOAKING TIME;
15 MINUTES FOR THE ROUILLE
COOKING TIME: 1 HOUR

Crab Bisque
SERVES 8

Prepare as for Classic Fish Soup, but after reheating stir in 200 g/7 oz cooked crab meat (fresh or canned), 150 ml/¼ pt/⅔ cup single (light) cream and 15 ml/1 tbsp brandy. Serve hot, with or without the rouille.

Thai Rice Cream Soup with Lime, Lemon Grass and Prawns

SERVES 6

A trendy soup in the Thai style.

1 stick of lemon grass, chopped
3 lime leaves
Juice of 1 lime
A 5 cm/2 in whole green chilli
4 garlic cloves
175 g/6 oz pork fillet, cut into strips
90 g/3½ oz/scant ½ cup Thai fragrant rice
400 g/14 oz/1 large can of coconut milk
1.5 litres/2½ pts/6 cups chicken stock
5 ml/1 tsp salt
25 g/1 oz coriander (cilantro) leaves
350 g/12 oz cooked, peeled prawns (shrimp)

① Place all the ingredients except half the coriander and the prawns in a large saucepan. Bring to the boil.

② Lower the heat, cover and simmer for 1 hour, stirring occasionally.

③ Leave to cool to lukewarm. Remove and discard the lime leaves.

④ Blend in two or three batches until fairly smooth, then transfer to a clean saucepan.

⑤ Reheat until hot, then add the prawns and warm through for 2 minutes.

⑥ Finely chop the remaining coriander and sprinkle over the soup to serve.

PREPARATION TIME: 15 MINUTES
COOKING TIME: 1¼ HOURS

Fast Seafood Soup
SERVES 4–6

A smart and surprisingly authentic-tasting fish soup, designed for slimmers.

2 × 185 g/2 × 6½ oz/2 small cans of tuna in brine
400 g/14 oz/1 large can of chopped tomatoes
30 ml/2 tbsp capers
2 garlic cloves, crushed
150 ml/¼ pt/⅔ cup dry white wine
30 ml/2 tbsp anchovy essence (extract)
10 ml/2 tsp cornflour (cornstarch)
15 ml/1 tbsp water
15–30 ml/1–2 tbsp chilli purée (paste)
15 ml/1 tbsp sun-dried tomato purée
Salt, to taste

① Tip the contents of the cans of tuna into the blender. Add the tomatoes, capers, garlic, wine and anchovy essence. Blend until very smooth and pour into a saucepan.

② Mix the cornflour smoothly with the water and add to the pan with the chilli and tomato purées.

③ Bring to the boil, stirring, then taste and add salt if necessary. Simmer gently for 4 minutes.

④ Serve very hot and, if liked, accompany with rouille (pages 102–3).

PREPARATION TIME: 10 MINUTES
COOKING TIME: 10 MINUTES

Smoked Haddock Cream Soup with Potatoes and Onions

SERVES 6

A silken-textured soup with a marked trace of smokiness coming through from the fish.

---

700 g/1½ lb potatoes, peeled and cubed
175 g/6 oz onions, thinly sliced
1.2 litres/2 pts/5 cups water
5 ml/1 tsp salt
450 g/1 lb smoked haddock fillet, skinned and cut into squares
90 ml/6 tbsp whipping cream
60 ml/4 tbsp chopped parsley

---

① Place the potatoes and onions in a saucepan with the water and salt. Bring to the boil.

② Lower the heat, cover and simmer for 40 minutes until the vegetables are very soft. Leave to cool to lukewarm.

③ Blend in two or three batches until smooth, then transfer to a clean saucepan.

④ Add the haddock and return the soup to the boil. Simmer for 2 minutes.

⑤ Remove from the heat and stir in the cream.

⑥ Serve very hot with a sprinkling of parsley on each portion.

PREPARATION TIME: 15 MINUTES
COOKING TIME: 50 MINUTES

Smoothies

Smoothies look something like thinned-down milkshakes in assorted colours – some dark, others light – and give spectacular flavour bursts of various fruits when they are sweet, or of mixed vegetables when savoury. They have taken off with the speed of lightning, are considered 'cool' and trendy and provide refreshing and nourishing drinks right through the year. They are also easy to make and, in some cases, purer and more economical than bought smoothies.

Milky Banana and Caramel Smoothie
SERVES 4

*A delicate-tasting smoothie with plenty of nourishment,
especially for youngsters.*

---

4 bananas, peeled
30 ml/2 tbsp caramel-flavoured syrup
10 ml/2 tsp grated orange rind
600 ml/1 pt/2½ cups full cream milk

---

① Break the banana flesh into the blender and add the remaining ingredients. Blend until smooth.

② Pour into a bowl or jug, cover and chill thoroughly.

③ Stir before serving in glasses or mugs.

PREPARATION TIME: 10 MINUTES

Pineapple, Lime and Apple Smoothie
SERVES 4

Flavour-wise, an adult affair with discretion.

---

1 large eating (dessert) apple, peeled, cored and quartered
½ large pineapple, peeled and flesh cubed
Juice of 1 lime
150 ml/¼ pt/⅔ cup water
300 ml/½ pt/1¼ cups tropical-style fruit juice
4 fresh mint leaves

---

① Cut the apple quarters into cubes and place in the blender with the remaining ingredients. Blend until smooth.

② Pour into a bowl or jug, cover and chill thoroughly.

③ Stir before serving in glasses or mugs.

PREPARATION TIME: 10 MINUTES

Strawberry and Orangeade Smoothie
SERVES 4

A smoothie with an intense strawberry flavour, supported by orange.

---

450 g/1 lb fresh strawberries, hulled
300 ml/½ pt/1¼ cups strawberry-flavoured yoghurt
350 ml/12 fl oz/1⅓ cups orangeade, chilled

---

① Place the strawberries and yoghurt in the blender and blend until smooth.

② Pour into a bowl or jug, cover and chill thoroughly.

③ Stir in the orangeade before serving in glasses or mugs.

PREPARATION TIME: 6 MINUTES

Strawberry, Orange and Pineapple Smoothie with Wine
SERVES 4–5

The summer is neatly wrapped up in this golden-red and dashing smoothie.

---

1 orange, peeled
450 g/1 lb strawberries, hulled
450 ml/¾ pt/2 cups pineapple juice
150 ml/¼ pt/⅔ cup red wine

---

① Separate the orange into segments and remove the pips.

② Place in the blender with the strawberries and half the pineapple juice. Blend until smooth.

③ Pour into a bowl or jug, then stir in the remaining pineapple juice and the wine. Cover and chill thoroughly.

④ Stir before serving in glasses or mugs.

PREPARATION TIME: 10 MINUTES

Strawberry and Peach Smoothie with Vanilla Ice and Rose Water

SERVES 5–6

This spells summer and is quite delicious.

450 g/1 lb strawberries, hulled
450 ml/¾ pt/2 cups peach juice
250 ml/8 fl oz/1 cup vanilla ice cream
15 ml/1 tbsp rose water

① Place the strawberries in the blender with half the peach juice, the ice cream and rose water. Blend until smooth.

② Pour into a bowl and add the remaining peach juice. Cover and chill for several hours.

③ Stir before serving in glasses or mugs.

PREPARATION TIME: 6 MINUTES

Nectarine, Blueberry and Custard Apple Juice Smoothie

SERVES 4–6

A harmonious smoothie in dark pink, freckled with blueberry seeds. The custard apple is also known as sour sop or guanabana and has a unique and distinctive taste.

3 ripe nectarines, halved and stoned (pitted)
250 g/9 oz blueberries
600 ml/1 pt/2½ cups custard apple juice

① Cut the nectarine halves into chunks and place in the blender with the blueberries and half the apple juice. Blend until smooth.

② Pour into a bowl and stir in the remaining apple juice. Cover and chill for several hours.

③ Stir before serving in glasses or mugs.

PREPARATION TIME: 5 MINUTES

Raspberry, Banana and Pink Grapefruit Smoothie

SERVES 4–5

This has an exquisite, semi-perfumed taste. A highly successful blend all round.

2 bananas, peeled
225 g/8 oz raspberries
30 ml/2 tbsp thick honey
600 ml/1 pt/2½ cups pink grapefruit juice

① Break the banana flesh into the blender and add the raspberries, honey and half the grapefruit juice. Blend until smooth.

② Pour into a bowl or jug and stir in the remaining grapefruit juice. Cover and chill thoroughly.

③ Stir before serving in glasses or mugs.

PREPARATION TIME: 5 MINUTES

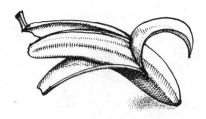

Mango, Mandarin Orange and Lemonade Smoothie

SERVES 3–4

All the ingredients work well together in this semi-tropical smoothie, with the delicious mango predominating.

2 ripe mangoes
300 g/11 oz/1 medium can of mandarin oranges in light syrup
300 ml/½ pt/1¼ cups lemonade

① Peel the mangoes and cut the flesh away from the stones (pits).

② Transfer the flesh to the blender and add the contents of the can of mandarins and half the lemonade. Blend until smooth.

③ Pour into a bowl or jug and stir in the remaining lemonade. Cover and chill thoroughly.

④ Stir before serving in glasses or mugs.

PREPARATION TIME: 5 MINUTES

Golden Plum and Apple Smoothie
SERVES 6

An autumnal (fall) smoothie with a subtle tang of breakfast marmalade.

---

700 g/1½ lb firm golden plums, halved and stoned (pitted)
200 g/7 oz/generous ½ cup coarse-cut dark orange marmalade
900 ml/1½ pts/3¾ cups apple juice

---

① Place the plums in a glass dish and stir in the marmalade.

② Microwave, uncovered, on full power for 8–10 minutes, stirring several times until tender. Leave to cool to lukewarm.

③ Transfer to the blender and add half the apple juice. Blend until smooth.

④ Pour into a bowl or jug and stir in the remaining apple juice. Cover and chill thoroughly.

⑤ Stir before serving in glasses or mugs.

PREPARATION TIME: 10 MINUTES
COOKING TIME: 10 MINUTES

Kiwi, Ginger and Lemon Smoothie
SERVES 3

A fluffy, pale green, tingling smoothie, speckled with kiwi seeds and refreshed with lemon sorbet.

---

4 kiwi fruit, peeled and thickly sliced
150 ml/¼ pt/⅔ cup water, chilled
60 ml/4 tbsp ginger and lemon grass cordial
250 ml/8 fl oz/1 cup lemon sorbet

---

① Blend all the ingredients until smooth.

② Pour into glasses and drink straight away.

PREPARATION TIME: 5 MINUTES

Rhubarb and Custard Smoothie with Elderflower

SERVES 4–5

All the fragrance of a country garden is captured in this old-fashioned style smoothie.

---

450 g/1 lb rhubarb, cut into pieces
300 ml/½ pt/1¼ cups water
60 ml/4 tbsp elderflower cordial
600 ml/1 pt/2½ cups sparkling elderflower drink
300 ml/½ pt/1¼ cups sweetened custard sauce

---

1. Place the rhubarb in a saucepan with the water. Cover and cook for 8 minutes or until the rhubarb is soft and pulpy. Leave to cool.

2. Transfer the rhubarb and cooking water to the blender. Add the elderflower cordial and half the elderflower drink and blend until smooth.

3. Pour into a bowl or jug and stir in the remaining elderflower drink and the custard sauce. Cover and chill thoroughly.

4. Stir before serving in glasses or mugs.

PREPARATION TIME: 10 MINUTES
COOKING TIME: 10 MINUTES

Melon and Ginger Smoothie
SERVES 4

*Cape Town is big on melon drinks and this smoothie is
adapted from one that was made up especially for me in a
city centre juice bar.*

---

350 g/12 oz honeydew melon flesh, diced
450 g/1 lb watermelon flesh, diced
150 ml/¼ pt/⅔ cup dry ginger ale

---

① Blend all the ingredients in two batches until smooth.

② Pour into a bowl, then cover and chill for several hours.

③ Stir before serving in glasses.

PREPARATION TIME: 10 MINUTES

Melon and Mango Smoothie with Orange Flower Water
SERVES 4

Exotic and exquisitely scented.

**1 charentais or cantaloupe melon, halved and seeded
(pitted)**
600 ml/1 pt/2½ cups mango juice
30 ml/2 tbsp orange flower water

---

① Scoop the melon flesh into the blender. Add the mango
juice and orange flower water and blend until smooth.

② Pour into a bowl, then cover and chill for several hours.

③ Stir before serving in glasses or mugs.

PREPARATION TIME: 7 MINUTES

Pineapple, Red Grape Juice and Campari Smoothie

SERVES 3

An adult smoothie in flamingo pink, tantalisingly laced with Campari.

450 g/1 lb pineapple flesh, cubed
300 ml/½ pt/1¼ cups sparkling red grape juice
30–60 ml/2–4 tbsp Campari

① Place all the ingredients in the blender and blend until very smooth.

② Strain to remove any fibrous pieces of pineapple remaining. Cover and chill.

③ Stir before serving in glasses or mugs.

PREPARATION TIME: 10 MINUTES

Pineapple, White Grape Juice and Crème de Menthe Smoothie

SERVES 3

A blessing after a heavy meal!

450 g/1 lb pineapple flesh, cubed
300 ml/½ pt/1¼ cups sparkling white grape juice
15–30 ml/1–2 tbsp crème de menthe

① Place all the ingredients in the blender and blend until very smooth.

② Strain to remove any fibrous pieces of pineapple remaining. Cover and chill.

③ Stir before serving in glasses or mugs.

PREPARATION TIME: 10 MINUTES

Fruit Cocktail and Passion Fruit Smoothie
SERVES 3–4

An absolutely stunning-tasting smoothie, crunchy with passion fruit seeds and coloured pale golden orange.

400 g/14 oz/1 large can of fruit cocktail
1 passion fruit, halved
300 ml/½ pt/1¼ cups passion fruit juice
45 ml/3 tbsp lemon juice

① Tip the contents of the can of fruit cocktail into the blender. Scoop the passion fruit pulp and seeds directly over the fruit cocktail.

② Add the passion fruit juice and lemon juice and blend until smooth.

③ Pour into a jug or bowl, cover and chill.

④ Stir before serving in glasses.

PREPARATION TIME: 7 MINUTES

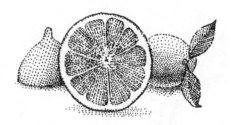

Citrus Smoothie
SERVES 4

A sparkling, rise-and-shine breakfast smoothie packed with good health and vitamin C. Use freshly squeezed orange juice if possible.

450 g/1 lb/1 very large can of grapefruit segments in juice or light syrup
Juice of 1 lime
Juice of 1 lemon
450 ml/¾ pt/2 cups fresh orange juice

① Tip the contents of the can of grapefruit segments into the blender.

② Add the three juices and blend until smooth. Cover and chill.

③ Stir before serving in glasses or mugs.

PREPARATION TIME: 10 MINUTES

Pineapple and Pear Smoothie

SERVES 4

A delicious cocktail of flavours to this smoothie, tinted orange with grenadine and very slightly sharp.

410 g/14½ oz/1 large can of pears in juice
600 ml/1 pt/2½ cups pineapple juice
15 ml/1 tbsp grenadine syrup
Juice of 1 lemon

① Tip the contents of the can of pears into the blender.

② Add the remaining ingredients and blend until smooth. Cover and chill.

③ Stir before serving in glasses or mugs.

PREPARATION TIME: 5 MINUTES

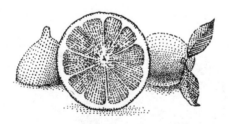

Curried Tomato and Mango Chutney Smoothie
SERVES 4

A stunning smoothie – rather like a tomato juice cocktail with an extra kick.

400 g/14 oz/1 large can of chopped tomatoes
300 ml/½ pt/1¼ cups water
45 ml/3 tbsp mango chutney
5 ml/1 tsp mild curry powder
25 g/1 oz coriander (cilantro) leaves
5 ml/1 tsp salt

① Tip the contents of the can of tomatoes into the blender.

② Add the remaining ingredients, adding salt to taste, and blend until smooth.

③ Pour into a bowl, then cover and chill for several hours.

④ Stir before serving in glasses or mugs

PREPARATION TIME: 5 MINUTES

Mock Bloody Mary
SERVES 4

Prepare as for Curried Tomato and Mango Chutney Smoothie, but stir a shot of ice-cold vodka into each glass.

Cucumber and Lime Smoothie
SERVES 3

The coolest of the cool and an idea passed on to me by a Caribbean acquaintance. You can have it either sweetened with sugar or salted; both taste great.

---

450 g/1 lb cucumber, peeled and cut into chunks
Juice of 1 lime
450 ml/¾ pt/2 cups iced water
5 ml/1 tsp salt
OR 10–15 ml/2–3 tsp caster (superfine) sugar

---

① Place all the ingredients in the blender and blend until completely smooth.

② Serve straight away in glasses.

PREPARATION TIME: 5 MINUTES

Beetroot, Orange and Yoghurt Smoothie

SERVES 4

A tingling, sweet-sour smoothie in brightest pink, based on the highly successful partnership of orange and beetroot (red beet).

350 g/12 oz sliced pickled beetroot
250 ml/8 fl oz/1 cup orange juice
300 ml/½ pt/1¼ cups water
5 ml/1 tsp salt
150 ml/¼ pt/⅔ cup plain yoghurt

① Blend all the ingredients in two batches in the blender.

② Pour into a bowl, cover and chill.

③ Stir before serving in glasses or mugs

PREPARATION TIME: 5 MINUTES

Index